Wisdom According to Paul in Relation to the Corinthian Problems

A Sociological and Rhetorical Analysis
of 1 Corinthians 1–4

Richard C. Rojas

ACADEMIC

© 2024 Richard C. Rojas

Published 2024 by Langham Academic
An imprint of Langham Publishing
www.langhampublishing.org

Langham Publishing and its imprints are a ministry of Langham Partnership

Langham Partnership
PO Box 296, Carlisle, Cumbria, CA3 9WZ, UK
www.langham.org

ISBNs:
978-1-83973-939-2 Print
978-1-78641-074-0 ePub
978-1-78641-075-7 PDF

Richard C. Rojas has asserted his right under the Copyright, Designs and Patents Act, 1988 to be identified as the Author of this work.

All rights reserved. No part of this publication may be reproduced, stored in a retrieval system or transmitted, in any form or by any means, electronic, mechanical, photocopying, recording or otherwise, without the prior written permission of the publisher or the Copyright Licensing Agency.

Requests to reuse content from Langham Publishing are processed through PLSclear. Please visit www.plsclear.com to complete your request.

All Scripture quotations, unless otherwise indicated, are taken from the New American Standard Bible®, Copyright © 1960, 1962, 1963, 1968, 1971, 1972, 1973, 1975, 1977, 1995, 2020 by The Lockman Foundation. Used by permission.

Scripture quotations marked (NIV) are taken from the Holy Bible, New International Version®, NIV®. Copyright © 1973, 1978, 1984, 2011 by Biblica, Inc.™ Used by permission of Zondervan.

British Library Cataloguing-in-Publication Data
A catalogue record for this book is available from the British Library

ISBN: 978-1-83973-939-2

Cover & Book Design: projectluz.com

Langham Partnership actively supports theological dialogue and an author's right to publish but does not necessarily endorse the views and opinions set forth here or in works referenced within this publication, nor can we guarantee technical and grammatical correctness. Langham Partnership does not accept any responsibility or liability to persons or property as a consequence of the reading, use or interpretation of its published content.

This solid study of 1 Corinthians 1–4 will orient you to the options that exist in our world: to pursue wisdom on our own, to focus on signs, or to see things as God does through his Spirit, where real wisdom lies. Using both rhetorical and sociological analysis of the text and working through the passage carefully, this book reflects solid engagement with the biblical message. I commend it to you.

Darrell Bock, PhD
Executive Director for Cultural Engagement, Hendricks Center,
Senior Research Professor of New Testament Studies,
Dallas Theological Seminary, Texas, USA

Dr. Richard C. Rojas's positioning of Paul's understanding of wisdom, and in particular, "Christ, the wisdom of God" in 1 Corinthians 1:24, becomes a heuristic tool for examining the argumentative interconnectedness of the problems in the church at Corinth that Paul addresses in 1 Corinthians 1–4. Dr. Rojas carefully engages a breadth of signal scholarship on 1 Corinthians 1–4. With clearly articulated exegesis as the methodological backbone, Dr. Rojas leverages sociological and rhetorical analyses to generate provocative questions to guide research. He includes, for example, discussion of the social classes of the congregation and the place of patronage. His eclectic approach to the rhetorical situation is informed both by Greco-Roman rhetoric and by modern practice, as seen in the landscape-shaping work of Finley, Judge, Bitzer, Meeks, and Theissen. In the context of Paul's overall engagement with the church, Dr. Rojas elucidates the message of 1 Corinthians 1–4 in a comprehensively broad, coherent argument. This work of critical scholarship is recommended for all specialists and non-specialist students of Saint Paul.

Kenneth A. Fox, PhD
Visiting Professor of New Testament,
Alliance Graduate School and Asia Graduate School of Theology, Philippines

Accurate interpretation of 1 Corinthians requires understanding both the social context of the church in Corinth and the rhetoric of Paul's response to the church's problems. Not least of these matters concerns the question of wisdom, both the worldly wisdom of the Corinthians and Paul's wisdom of the cross and the spirit. Rojas's judicious and painstaking sociological and rhetorical analysis of 1 Corinthians 1–4 shines a light not only on the exegesis of the letter but also on boasting, divisions, and following Jesus Christ in every age.

Brian S. Rosner, PhD
Principal,
Ridley College, Australia

Dr. Rojas demonstrates the interconnection between the problems of church division, boastful pride, and human wisdom within the church in Corinth, problems that Paul found it necessary to address and correct in 1 Corinthians 1–4. Such problems, of course, still plague the church today – divisions within churches have obviously not disappeared. The solution, as Dr. Rojas explains, is the wisdom of God embodied in Christ and revealed by the spirit. Dr. Rojas's book is worth reading for its detailed explanation of the social context and rhetorical situation in the church in Corinth, but more than that, it is worth reading for the way in which it challenges our own false sense of superiority and our own failure to seek after the wisdom of God.

Joel F. Williams, PhD
Professor of New Testament Studies,
Biblical Seminary of the Philippines

For Kim (Pearl Anne), Jaci, and Chad

Contents

Acknowledgments ix

Abstract xi

Abbreviations xiii

Chapter 1 1
   Introduction
   1.1 State of the Question 2
   1.2 Research Problem 15
   1.3 Methodology 16
      1.3.1 The Method of Sociological Interpretation 17
      1.3.2 The Rhetorical Method 26
   1.4 Overview of the Study and Application of the Method to
       the Study 41

Chapter 2 43
   The Social Context of the Corinthian Church
   2.1 The Social Profile of Roman Corinth 43
   2.2 The Social Structure in Roman Corinth 54
   2.3 Patronage in Roman Corinth 61
   2.4 Sophistic Movement in Roman Corinth during the
       First Century 69
   2.5 Summary 74

Chapter 3 77
   Rhetorical Analysis of 1 Corinthians 1–4
   3.1 The Rhetorical Unit 77
   3.2 The Rhetorical Situation 78
      3.2.1 The Exigencies in 1 Corinthians 1–4 78
      3.2.2 The Audience in 1 Corinthians 1–4 86
      3.2.3 The Constraints in 1 Corinthians 1–4 87
   3.3 Species of Rhetoric and Stasis Theory 88
      3.3.1 Species of Rhetoric 88
      3.3.2 Stasis Theory 89
   3.4 Invention, Style, and Arrangement 90
      3.4.1 The *Exordium*: 1 Corinthians 1:4–9 90
      3.4.2 The *Propositio*: 1 Corinthians 1:10 91
      3.4.3 The *Narratio*: 1 Corinthians 1:11–17 92

Abstract

This study seeks to establish the relationship of Paul's wisdom teaching to the problems of the Corinthian church in 1 Corinthians 1–4. Scholars (such as Hurd, Dahl, and Fee) initially propose how these problems are related and how Paul's teaching on wisdom may further clarify the relevance of Paul's response to the entire issue. I seek to develop this.

In this research, I aim to find out how Paul's wisdom teaching that comes to expression here connects with the problems of division, wisdom, and boasting. There are three aspects of this study that I will explore. First, I will investigate the contextual background of wisdom in 1 Corinthians 1–4. Second, I will find out the meaning of Paul's wisdom concept, in particular, "Christ, the wisdom of God." Third, I will explore how Paul's wisdom teaching can provide a key for exploring how the three problems connect. In this study, I provide a sociological and rhetorical analysis of the text. I combine this with an exegesis of 1 Corinthians 1–4 seen against Paul's correspondence with the Corinthian church.

The Corinthian believers thought the wisdom of the world makes them wise but the opposite is true. As shown by their conduct, they are foolish. Their foolishness is manifested in their boastings and quarreling that leads to division. The problem of division is caused by the problem of boasting, which is rooted in the problem of wisdom. Paul's wisdom teaching addresses the root cause of the exigencies in the church, the problem of wisdom. Paul taught them they could only become wise by embracing Christ, the wisdom of God, revealed through the Holy Spirit. As such, they must stop boasting about themselves, Apollos, or Paul. Their boasting is divisive and it betrays the implication of the message of the cross that unites those who believe – whether Jews or Greeks, eloquent or not, wise, noble, powerful, or weak. In the wisdom of God there is no division respective of race, ethnicity, and skills in human persuasiveness (eloquence in rhetoric). Every believer belongs to Christ and there is no reason to boast, quarrel, or be divided. As people of the wisdom of God, they must choose to be in one mind and intention to keep the unity of the body of Christ.

Abbreviations

Aristotle, *Rhet.*	Aristotle, *Art of Rhetoric*
BDAG	Bauer, W. *A Greek-English Lexicon of the New Testament and Other Early Christian Literature.* Revised and edited by Frederick William Danker. 3rd ed. Chicago: University of Chicago Press, 2000.
Cicero, *De or.*	Cicero, *De Oratore*
Cicero, *Tusc. Disp.*	Cicero, *Tusculian Disputations*
Dio Chrysostom, *Or.*	Dio Chrysostom, *Discourses 1–11*
Dio Chrysostom, [*Cor.*]	Dio Chrysostom, *Discourses 37–60*
Philo, *De Leg*	Philo, *De Legatione ad Gaium*
Philostratus, *Vit. Soph.*	Philostratus, *Vitae Sophistarum*
Quintilian, *Inst.*	Quintilian, *Institutio Oratoria*
Strabo, *Geogr.*	Strabo, *Geography*

CHAPTER 1

Introduction

Many studies have been done to reconstruct the situation in 1 Corinthians 1–4. These works have given us valuable insights into the nature of the problems Paul faced in Corinth, namely, the problem of division, problem of boasting, and problem of wisdom. The problem of division refers to the quarreling in the church that has caused a rift in the relationships of the members of the Corinthian church. The problem of boasting refers to Corinthian members of the church who are boasting not only about their preferred missionary workers but also about themselves. They have become puffed up and jealous of one another. Their boasting and jealousy have caused quarrels among them. The problem of wisdom refers to Corinthian believers' faulty understanding of what it means to be wise. The Corinthian believers thought they could be wise by pursuing the wisdom of the world. In their context, this refers to the pursuit of acquiring knowledge and skills so that one becomes eloquent in rhetoric or skillful in human persuasiveness. As such, they gained a false sense of superiority because they thought they had already reached the pinnacle of wisdom by attaining the wisdom of the world.

While the different views of scholars on this matter opened up various breakthroughs in academic research, there remains an essential element of study that deserves further attention, the relationship of Paul's wisdom teaching to the problems of division, boasting, and wisdom in the Corinthian church in 1 Corinthians 1–4.

At the outset, it must be noted that this study assumes the unity and integrity of 1 Corinthians. This approach is consistent with my method – a sociological and rhetorical analysis of the relationship of Paul's wisdom teaching in relation to the problems in 1 Corinthians 1–4. Also, this study will not address related issues discussed by Paul outside of 1 Corinthians 1–4. For example, in 1 Corinthians 1–4 Paul addresses the problems of division and boasting. In 1 Corinthians 11, Paul refers to the division using the same word σχίσματα that he uses in 1 Corinthians 1:10. Paul also refers to the arrogant attitude of the Corinthian believers in 1 Corinthians 5 in view of the fornication that they tolerated in the church. These related issues may be examined as a continuation of research in view of the arguments I present in this study, particularly the relationship of Paul's wisdom teaching to the problems in 1 Corinthians 1–4. Finally, it is noted here that there is a lack of scholarship devoted to the study of the relevance of Paul's wisdom teaching in relation to the problems of division, boasting, and wisdom in 1 Corinthians 1–4. Thus, this study offers a sociological and rhetorical analysis of 1 Corinthians 1–4 that seeks to establish the relationship of Paul's wisdom teaching to the Corinthian problems in 1 Corinthians 1–4.

1.1 State of the Question

The following review shows how select scholars have connected Paul's wisdom concept to the Corinthian problems in 1 Corinthians 1–4.

F. C. Baur says that Paul deals with a divided church that is also questioning his apostolic authority.[1] According to Baur, Paul is defending his apostolic ministry against his "Judaizing opponents" who are dividing the church. The problem revolves around the factionalism that is expressed in the slogans of 1 Corinthians 1:12, suggesting the parties of Paul, Apollos, Cephas, and Christ. Baur says it is not difficult to accept that Corinthian believers would consider themselves as followers of Paul and Apollos. Paul affirms that he and Apollos are "coworkers with God" in Corinth (1 Cor 3:9). Peter's influence may have reached the Corinthian church though he did not visit Corinth; and the Cephas party recognize him as their chief. What about the Christ party? According to Baur, these are the Jewish believers who consider themselves more significant than the Gentile believers because of their direct link to Christ. They claim Christ came for the Jews thus Christ belongs to them.[2]

---

1. This section is based on Baur, *Paul the Apostle*, 268–320. See also Baur, "Two Epistles," 51–60.

2. Baur, *Paul the Apostle*, 269–78.

Baur argues that the four slogans do not represent four parties. Paul uses the four slogans to emphasize the divisions in the church. For Baur, the conflict is between two parties, the Pauline party (of Paul and Apollos) and Petrine party (of Cephas and Christ). Paul has no known conflict with Apollos. It follows that there is no cause for conflict to arise between their faithful followers so they actually belong to one party, the Pauline party. On the other hand, the Petrine party is composed of the Cephas party and Christ party. The Petrine party considers Peter as occupying the highest position among the apostles because he was one of the three disciples closest to Christ.[3]

According to Baur, the factionalism in the Corinthian church is rooted in their gentile (Pauline party) and Jewish (Petrine party) heritages. The Petrine party had a "special zeal . . . for the mosaic law,"[4] which they could not have freely practiced in a gentile church planted by Paul who had "a critical stance toward the law."[5] Also, they question the genuineness of Paul's apostolic authority because he was not a disciple of Jesus during his earthly life, which was considered one of "the most essential requirements of true apostolic authority."[6] They could not attribute to him the apostolic authority equal to that of Peter and other disciples due to his lack of connection with Jesus.[7]

Thus, Baur argues that in 1 Corinthians 1–4 Paul is not only addressing factionalism in the church but also defending his apostleship against those who questioned it.[8] According to Baur, Paul asserts that their love for the wisdom of the world and carnal minds have caused the strife among them. Thus, the Corinthian believers are not qualified to judge or examine their leaders. Instead, they must examine themselves.[9]

Baur establishes the identity of the Pauline party and the Apollos party but fails to provide sufficient argument for the Cephas party and Christ party. In the same manner, Baur fails to establish from the text that the Pauline party and the Petrine party existed. Also, Baur's claim that Paul is defending his apostleship from those people who questioned it lacks evidence from

---

3. Baur, 274–78.
4. Baur, 277.
5. Adams and Horrell, *Christianity at Corinth*, 14.
6. Baur, *Paul the Apostle*, 304.
7. Baur, 276–77.
8. Baur, 276–80, 304.
9. Baur, 307.

1 Corinthians 1–4. As I will explain further below, there is no direct accusation against Paul in 1 Corinthians 1–4 that is related to his apostleship.

Johannes Munck, in contrast, claims that there was neither factionalism nor differences in doctrine.[10] Munck points out that Paul did not use the Greek word for faction, αἱρέσις, which is usually used in an eschatological sense – as in 1 Corinthians 11:19, the book of Acts, and other books in the New Testament. In this sense, Munck suggests that factions denote a more "lasting separation" in the future.[11] Thus, the situation in the Corinthian church was not "yet a matter of factions" but a temporal state where believers could not be of the same mind about important matters in the church.[12] Instead, Paul describes the situation in the Corinthian church as σχίσματα in 1 Corinthians 1:10, which is a case of bickering and disunity. Munck takes us to the Gospel of John where the word σχίσματα is used to refer to a form of disagreement over an issue covering a short period of time (John 7:43; 9:16; 10:19). Further, in 1 Corinthians 11:18 Munck says the word refers to the forming of cliques whenever people gather for the common meal. In particular the rich and poor are distinctly separated from each other. In 1 Corinthians 12:25 Munck also argues that cliques were formed because of what they perceived to be an unequal distribution of the gifts of the Holy Spirit. In view of all these usages, Munck proposes that the problem in the Corinthian church in 1 Corinthians 1–4 is not a matter of factions but division among church members over non-theological issues. In addition, Munck observes that in 1 Corinthians 1:11 Paul describes the current situation in the church as ἔριδες. People are bickering and fighting with each other on issues relating to their leaders. Paul is not indicating that they were currently divided but that they must stop this bickering to avoid dividing the church.[13]

Munck notes that it is difficult to prove the existence of four different factions in 1 Corinthians. It is true that various problems plagued the church in 1 Corinthians 1–4 but it is not clear how these problems connect to the four factions. Munck asserts that if the four factions exist, there should be references to them in the rest of the letter. If there is a Paul faction, how can

---

10. This section is based from Munck, *Paul*, 135–67.
11. Munck, *Paul*, 136.
12. Munck, 137.
13. Munck, 137–139.

Paul rebuke the people who are supporting him? If there is a Cephas faction, its connection to questioning Paul's apostleship is not clear. Munck notes Paul's strong words, "For no one can lay any foundation other than the one already laid, which is Jesus Christ" (1 Cor 3:11 NIV). Munck suggests that Paul is perhaps attacking a misunderstanding of the words of Jesus about Peter, "on this rock I will build my church" (Matt 16:18 NIV). Munck admits, though, that it is uncertain not only whether the Cephas faction existed but also whether they misunderstood the word of Jesus about Peter being the rock. If there is a Christ faction, the only evidence showing their existence is the mention of them by name. To suppose, as Baur did, that this group was composed of Jewish believers claiming a direct connection to Jesus lacks any support outside Baur's imagination. Munck notes that in 2 Corinthians 10:7–10 the phrase Χριστοῦ εἶναι seems to allude to the Christ faction but many scholars agree (e.g. Windisch, Strachan, Bachmann, Plummer) that this refers to the usual sense "to be a Christian/apostle." If there is an Apollos faction, how can Paul attack the followers of a co-worker whom he regards as a loyal and faithful servant of the Lord Jesus Christ? It cannot be established firmly whether Apollos or his followers are the ones being addressed by Paul in 1 Corinthians 1:18–21 since there is no reference that points Apollos or his followers are seeking worldly wisdom.[14]

So, if there are no factions as Munck asserts, to whom does Paul address his teachings? What is Paul's argument in this section? Munck proposes the following. First, Paul is not addressing Jewish wisdom because it is evident that the Jews are not seeking wisdom but signs, as indicated in 1 Corinthians 1:22–24. Second, Paul is not addressing particular people or groups mention in 1 Corinthians 1:12 but the church as a whole. Rather, Paul is addressing the "I belong to" attitude of the Corinthian believers in relation to how they esteem their leaders whom they supposed to be the source of their wisdom. This attitude causes them to highly exalt themselves. In 1 Corinthians 3 Paul confronts this "I belong to" attitude by emphasizing that every leader whom the Lord used in building the Corinthian church is God's servant. No one stands supreme above the others for they are all co-workers. None of them

---

14. Munck, 139–44.

should be considered as their foundation regardless of their role and contribution in their lives for Christ is the true foundation.[15]

Third, Paul is not confronting a doctrinal or theological problem. No doctrinal issue comes to expression in 1 Corinthians 1–4. As noted above, there are no factions in the church. As such, there are no hints pointing to issues being represented or advocated by each faction even outside 1 Corinthians 1–4.[16] Fourth, Paul addresses their erroneous understanding of the gospel, their leaders, and themselves. Munck notes that the Corinthian believers regard the "Christian message as wisdom like that of the Greeks."[17] Munck explains that, based on Paul's argument in 1 Corinthians 2:6–16, the message of wisdom they proclaim to the mature is not the wisdom of the world. It is "expressed in a mystery" that cannot be discerned by the wisdom of the world or by the unspiritual for it is foolishness to them but discerned only by the Spirit of God whom God gives to believers.[18] Also, they regard their leaders as wisdom teachers. In 1 Corinthians 2:1 Paul argues that they are not wisdom teachers because when he came, he did not proclaim using the wisdom of the world or by persuasive words but by the Spirit's power. In 1 Corinthians 3:6–9 Paul explains that they are all co-laborers with Christ. Paul's role was to plant the seed and Apollos's role was to water it but ultimately, it was God who caused the growth. Finally, the Corinthian believers regard themselves as wise. They are boasting about their wisdom and their wise leaders whom they consider wisdom teachers. In 1 Corinthians 1:26–31 Paul confronts them saying none of them is wise (based on worldly standards) before they were in Christ. They did not possess any wisdom before the gospel was preached to them. He exhorts them in 1 Corinthians 2:6–16 about the wisdom of God that is received through the Holy Spirit. Since this is a gift from God, they need not boast about it or themselves. This wisdom is for the mature, not for the unspiritual, which Paul thinks they are because of the division and bickering in the church. Paul also points out that there is no reason to boast about their leaders whom they thought to be wise because they are God's

---

15. Munck, 148–52.
16. Munck, 152
17. Munck, 152.
18. Munck, 155–57.

servants whom the Lord has tasked to build the church and whom God will judge at the proper time.[19]

Munck's claim that there are no factions and his recognition that they are quarreling and disunited are difficult to reconcile. If they are quarreling and disunited, how can there be no factions? In fact, he alludes to the existence of cliques that are quarreling against each other. If these cliques are quarreling, how can these not be factions?

In addition, Munck cannot base his conclusion about σχίσματα from 1 Corinthians 11:18 and use it to assert the nonexistence of groups in 1 Corinthians 1:10. The σχίσματα in 1 Corinthians 11:18 refers to differences among the members of the group (cliques) over their common meal practices. Here, the tension exists internally between members of the groups (cliques) whereas the tension in 1 Corinthians 1:10 exists externally between groups.

Munck is correct when he said that it is difficult to establish the existence of the factions because there are no other references to the Paul, Apollos, Cephas, and Christ groups outside of 1 Corinthians 1–4. However, I do not agree with him that it is difficult to establish the connection between the problems of the church to the factions, if indeed, they exist. Munck affirms that they are quarreling and boasting about their leaders so the connection is very clear.

John C. Hurd, Jr., in his book *The Origin of 1 Corinthians*, notes that the issues Paul addresses in 1 Corinthians 1–4 are either issues that did not bother the Corinthian believers (they did not seem to realize it to be damaging or wrong) or issues they did not want Paul to know or respond to. Otherwise, they should have included it in their official letter they sent through Stephanas, Fortunatus, and Achaicus to inquire about certain issues affecting the church.[20]

According to Hurd, Paul is addressing two important issues (only) in 1 Corinthians 1–4: the party division and the problem of wisdom. On party division, Paul knows that the situation poses a damaging effect to the church. They have become proud and are quarreling among themselves. Thus, Paul is compelled to confront it directly.[21] There seems to be an allusion to the dif-

---

19. Munck, 157–67.
20. Hurd, *Origin*, 75.
21. Hurd, *Origin*, 75–76.

ferent groups in 1 Corinthians 1:12 but there are no other references about these groups outside of 1 Corinthians 1–4.[22]

Hurd notes that there seems to be an indication that Paul is defending himself from an attack on his apostleship in 1 Corinthians 9. However, Paul's statements in 1 Corinthians 9 "is not a defence against an attack on Paul's apostleship but is his defence against a challenge, real or imagined to what he considers his rights as an apostle."[23] There is no evidence to show though that Paul's apostolic authority is being questioned by the Corinthians believers. The fact that they sent a delegation to inquire from him about some matters concerning the church shows they are still upholding his authority (cf. 1 Cor 11:2). There is no previous encounter showing any cause that might have damaged their relationships. On a deeper level though, Hurd suggests there is possibility their relationships have been "somewhat strained" as indicated by Paul's stern rebuke (see 1 Cor 4:8, 10; 5:6; 14:36).[24] They have become proud and are quarreling among themselves. Paul is compelled to confront it directly and uncompromisingly. Paul may have sounded like he is attacking the church but his tone is exercised within the context of being their spiritual father (1 Cor 4:14–15).

On the problem of wisdom, Hurd notes that the church misunderstood what true wisdom is. The Corinthian believers consider themselves as wise "beyond the ordinary."[25] Paul responds by emphasizing that the message of the cross is superior to the wisdom of the world (1 Cor 1:18–2:5).[26]

Hurd observes that Paul seems to take these two problems as one because his discussion on division is interspersed with the discussion of wisdom. Thus, he suggests these two problems may be treated as one problem with two aspects.[27] In asserting that there are only two problems in the church, Hurd fails to notice the efforts Paul has devoted to addressing the problem of boasting in 1 Corinthians 3 and 4. Paul's extensive discussion of the problem of boasting in 1 Corinthians 3 and 4 clearly indicates that he treats the problem of boasting separate from the problem of division. Also, I do not agree

---

22. Hurd, 96.
23. Hurd, 110.
24. Hurd, 111.
25. Hurd, 76.
26. Hurd, 76.
27. Hurd, 77.

with Hurd that these problems may be treated as one problem. However, I argue that they are inter-related.

Nils Dahl notes that the church is burdened with the presence of quarreling (ἔριδες) in 1 Corinthians 1:11, jealousy and strife in 1 Corinthians 3:3–4 (ζῆλος καὶ ἔρις), and boasting (ἐφυσιώθησάν) in 1 Corinthians 4:18.[28] Also, the problems in the Corinthian church are related with the assumption that Paul is not coming back to Corinth (1 Cor 4:18).[29] He observes that among the problems in the church the key issue revolves around the problem involving the relationship between Paul and the Corinthian believers. Here, he agrees with Baur that Paul is defending his apostolic ministry, which Munck and Hurd fail to take into account.[30]

Dahl asserts that there are criticisms hurled against Paul as implied in 1 Corinthians 4:3. There are various probabilities of the content of the criticisms. Some of them could be deduced from Paul's statement that gives hint to his lack of rhetorical ability such as in 1 Corinthians 1:17 ("not in cleverness of speech"), 2:1 ("not in superiority of speech or of wisdom"), and 2:4 ("not in persuasive words of wisdom"). In addition, in 1 Corinthians 3:1 and 3:18 the Corinthian believers think they are wise and spiritual people so they consider Paul is not a spiritual person because he does not possess the superior wisdom like them. Further, Paul's claims in 1 Corinthians 4:9–13 also add to the criticisms especially when he declares that he and the other apostles are "fools for Christ," "weak," "without honor," "homeless," "reviled," and "slandered."[31]

In addition, Dahl also suggests that the quarreling in the church is related to the opposition and criticism against Paul. It is noted that the church at Corinth sent Stephanas, Fortunatus, and Achaicus to bring a letter to Paul to ask him of his opinion on certain matters and to communicate to him that they continue to hold on to the traditions that he passed on to them (1 Cor 11:2). Paul, however, is aware of the quarreling in the church and opposition against him through the oral reports from the household of Chloe. Dahl observes that there is a seeming disconnect between the oral reports that Paul

---

28. Dahl, "Paul and the Church," 318.
29. Dahl, "Paul and the Church," 318.
30. Dahl, "Paul and the Church," 317.
31. Dahl, 321–22.

heard and the letter brought by Stephanas. Since the report about the quarrel and opposition did not come through Stephanas, it is believed that though Stephanas learned about it, it got worse only after Stephanas and his group had left Corinth. Dahl theorizes that the quarrel stems from the fact that some people objected to the idea of asking Paul's opinion on the matters being raised in the letter. Based on the attitude of the Corinthian believers towards Paul as mentioned above, they opposed and questioned the idea because they did not consider him as a person with apostolic authority. Instead, they were hoping that Cephas or Apollos would have been consulted on those matters.[32] Within this context, Dahl proposes that the slogans in 1 Corinthians 1:12 were all "declarations of independence from Paul" by the different parties except the Paul party who are believed to be loyal to Paul and who esteemed him more highly than others ("I belong to Paul").[33] Thus, everyone is saying, except the Paul party, we have nothing to do with Paul.

According to Dahl, Paul addresses the whole church instead of the different parties and carefully articulates his defense in 1 Corinthians 1–4 to avoid any accusation that he was favoring any party in the church and to avoid more quarreling that might lead to division. He establishes his role as a wise builder, apostle, and spiritual father of them all not just of some of the groups, particularly not of those loyal to him. Thus, he begins this section with an appeal to stop quarreling and avoid division in the church. He also clarifies that there is no tension between him, Apollos, and Cephas because they are all co-laborers in the Lord and all belong to Christ. Thus, the quarreling about their leaders is baseless and unnecessary. He also shows that what they perceive as a sign of lack of wisdom is actually a demonstration that the gospel he preaches is not based on him but on the power of God (1 Cor 2:1–5). On the other hand, Paul also establishes that he is, indeed, an apostle who deserves their respect and recognition (1 Cor 3:10–11; 4:15). If he were less than an apostle compared to their leaders, how could he lay the foundation as a wise builder from which Cephas and Apollos built on that foundation with their ministry? Dahl notes that in Paul's defense he did not only assert his qualifications as an apostle but also points out how the Corinthian believers have failed to grasp the truth about their claims that

---

32. Dahl, 322–325.
33. Dahl, 322.

they are spiritual and wise. The Corinthian believers have misunderstood the theology of the cross. They claim to have wisdom of their own (apart from Christ) but do not understand the true wisdom, Christ, the wisdom of God. They think they possess power and glory but they do not recognize that the glory of Christ is found in weakness and sufferings (1 Cor 4:9–13). They pass judgment on their leaders but do not realize they are not qualified to do it because they are unspiritual and unwise. They boast of their spirituality but their conduct contradicts their claim.[34]

Dahl notes that Paul encloses this whole section with two appeals in 1 Corinthians 1:10 and 4:16 as indicated by παρακαλῶ. This is a Pauline formula used to communicate Paul's emphasis that the Corinthian believers must agree with one another to avoid division (1 Cor 1:10) and to imitate Paul (1 Cor 4:6). This Pauline formula is different from the "strict imperatives" as this is carried out as a "voluntary response," not as a strict compliance to a certain command. In both appeals, Paul "wants his converts not only to stand firm, in the Lord, but also in their loyalty to him."[35]

In summary, Dahl reiterates that 1 Corinthians 1–4 is Paul's defense of his apostolic authority. Also, the quarrels among them are linked to their opposition to Paul and to the decision to inquire from Paul about some issues. Finally, Dahl writes,

> 1 Corinthians 1:10–4:21 not only has the function of re-establishing the authority of Paul as the founder and father of the entire church at Corinth, but also prepares for the content of the answers given to the questions raised and indicates the theological basis from which these answers are given.[36]

Dahl proposes four issues in this controversy: the problem of the quarrels that resulted to division; the problem of wisdom ("power and wisdom of God over against the wisdom of men"); the problem of boasting in relation to their teachers and themselves; and the problem of Paul's relationship with the Corinthian believers.[37] Dahl sees a clear connection between the problems of quarreling and boasting (they are quarreling because they boast over their

---

34. Dahl, 331–32.
35. Knox, *Life of Paul*, 95, quoted by Dahl, "Paul and the Church," 319–20.
36. Dahl, "Paul and the Church," 333–34.
37. Dahl, 320.

teachers/leaders), but he is uncertain how the problem of wisdom connects with the problems of quarreling, boasting, and Paul's relationship with the Corinthian believers. Among the four issues, Dahl considers Paul's defense of his apostolic authority as the overarching point of discussion because it not only re-establishes his apostolic authority but also his integrity in answering their official queries.[38]

Gordon Fee admits that the church is divided internally as manifested by their quarreling. However, Fee asserts that the greater problem is not the internal quarreling but their attitude toward Paul and the gospel he preaches.[39] There is tension in the relationship between Paul and some of the leaders of the church who are advocating "an anti-Pauline view of things."[40] They doubt whether Paul has the authority to give them counsel about the issues the church is facing. Fee suggests the possibility that through Apollos's ministry some Corinthian believers consider their "new faith in terms of sophia (wisdom), as though, in comparison with others, it were the ultimate expression of divine sophia."[41] Thus, they think they are already mature. So, they consider the content of Paul's message as "milk" suited only for those who are still new in their faith. Likewise, they question his lack of rhetorical skills, which they think manifest that Paul lacks wisdom.[42]

Fee believes that the Corinthian church had a theological problem. As noted above, the Corinthian believers apparently have misunderstood what it means to be spiritual and this has affected how they view Paul's authority (as their founder/apostle) and the gospel he preached to them. They assume they are already spiritual so they consider Paul's gospel as only for the non-spiritual or immature, spiritual milk for babies (1 Cor 2:6; 3:1).[43]

In relation to this theological problem is what Fee calls "spiritualized eschatology."[44] It asserts the fact that though they are still in the body ("not yet"), they "are already experiencing the Spirit in full measure," ("already")

---

38. Dahl, 320–21.
39. Fee, *First Epistle*, 6.
40. Fee, 6.
41. Fee, 8.
42. Fee, 8–9.
43. Fee, 10
44. Fee, 12

Introduction 13

thus they are the "spiritual ones."⁴⁵ This is related to their enthusiasm in the gift of tongues where they believe that if one has the gift of tongues, they have reached the level of spirituality where they have already "assumed the spiritual existence of the angels."⁴⁶ Fee writes, "If tongues is understood as the 'language of angels,' then their experience of glossolalia is evidence for them that they have already arrived (already they speak the language of heaven)."⁴⁷

Fee suggests four issues in the Corinthian church. First, there is the issue on quarreling among the members regarding their loyalty to their respective leaders. Second, there is the issue of wisdom where Corinthian wisdom is thought to be superior to Paul's wisdom. Third, there is an issue on boasting about them (1 Cor 1:29–31; 3:21; 4:7). And finally, there is the issue on the tension that exists between Paul and the church.⁴⁸ Fee suggests a possibility of linking these four issues together. Fee's view, which he labels "largely speculative," suggests that the problem of wisdom is a result of the Hellenistic influence where the emphasis focuses more on "polished oration than with significant content . . . [that] had perhaps led the Corinthians themselves to begin to think of their new-found faith as an expression of sophia – the divine sophia, to be sure, but sophia nonetheless."⁴⁹ Fee suggests that probably this is the cause of their quarreling and boasting, creating tension in the church. More importantly, according to Fee, this has posed a significant threat to the gospel that Paul preached, to the church, and to Paul's apostolic ministry. Fee suggests that Paul's main concern was not the division in the church but the Corinthians' "false theology, which had exchanged the theology of the cross for a false triumphalism that went beyond, or excluded, the cross."⁵⁰

Baur, Dahl, and Fee assert that Paul is defending his apostolic authority against his critics. Baur's assertion that some believers in Corinth, whom Baur proposes as members of the Petrine party, are questioning his authority because of his lack of connection to Christ is not warranted in the text. There is nothing in 1 Corinthians 1–4 that shows this notion exists. Dahl and Fee share similar ideas in raising the issue of the probability that there

---

45. Fee, 12
46. Fee, 11–12.
47. Fee, 12.
48. Fee, 48–49.
49. Fee, 49.
50. Fee, 49–50.

are people influencing some of the members of the church to question his authority. However, there is no clear indication that the Corinthian believers are actually doing this. In addition, there is also no reference to Paul's attempt to explain the nature of his apostolic authority or defend it.[51] Dahl is correct when he points out that the Corinthian believers are criticizing Paul. However, Dahl has not shown how the criticisms can be considered an attack on Paul's apostolic authority. Perhaps Dahl is looking at the possible echoes of what the Corinthian believers could be saying about the situation.[52] In this section Paul is quite clear when he wants to address specific statements that the Corinthian believers are saying either against him or against one another. In 1 Corinthians 1:12 Paul says, "Each one of you is saying, 'I am of Paul,' and 'I of Apollos,' and 'I of Cephas,' and 'I of Christ.'" The same formula is used in 1 Corinthians 3:3, "For when one says, 'I am of Paul,' and another, 'I am of Apollos.'" In the references mentioned by Dahl (1 Cor 1:17; 2:1, 4; 3:2, and 4:3), Paul's statements denote that he is addressing the criticism about his rhetorical skills but there is no indication that he is trying to defend his authority. In 1 Corinthians 4:18 Paul points out it has reached his attention that someone was saying he is not coming to visit Corinth. Based on this pattern when Paul wants to address a certain accusation or statement of the Corinthian believers, he either refers to it specifically or alludes to it with an explanation. Now, if indeed the Corinthian believers are attacking his apostolic authority, it is expected that Paul would have defended himself, especially as these accusations are directed not only to him as a person but to his apostolic authority and the gospel he preaches. Fee's assertion that the priority exigency Paul needs to modify is not the division between the groups in the church but between the church and Paul is difficult to establish. There is no reference from the text that this is Paul's priority in writing the letter. In the same manner, it is difficult to tie Fee's view that the Corinthian believers have managed to maintain a non-hostile relationship with Paul and are still predisposed to listen to him even when they are questioning his apostolic authority.

---

51. Cf. Given, *Paul's True Rhetoric*, 94.

52. Cf. Brookins, "Wise Corinthians," 51–76; Hurd, *Origin*, 107; Baird, "One Against the Other," 119; Goodrich, *Paul as an Administrator*, 122.

The Corinthian believers may be criticizing Paul but it does not mean they are questioning his authority. Paul's combative tone in the whole section where he rebukes the Corinthian believers and even alludes to a church leader in 1 Corinthians 4:21 precisely demonstrates that his apostolic authority remains unquestioned. Otherwise, Paul would not have the boldness to assert his role as their spiritual father and apostle of the Lord Jesus Christ. The fact that Paul exhorts them to imitate him demonstrates that his apostolic authority remains unchallenged despite the seeming tension between them. In addition, the church's decision to inquire from him reflects that they still recognize his apostolic authority.

In discussing the problems of the Corinthian church in 1 Corinthians 1–4 the views of these scholars initially propose how these problems are related and how Paul's teaching on wisdom may further clarify the relevance of Paul's response to the entire issue. With these discussions in view, I will build upon and develop the issues. A fresh reexamination of this well-ploughed text through the lens of this question may shed new insights into the issue: Can Paul's wisdom teaching provide a lens for seeing how the problem of division, problem of wisdom, and problem of boasting connect together?

1.2 Research Problem

In 1 Corinthians 1–4 Paul confronts three problems that are somehow linked: division, boasting, and wisdom. In this research, I seek to find out how Paul's wisdom teaching that comes to expression here connects with the problems of division, wisdom, and boasting. In addressing these issues, Paul responds by teaching about what true wisdom is. In this section, it is obvious how Paul placed emphasis on the discussion of wisdom in relation to the ongoing tension in the church.

At this preliminary stage, there are three aspects of this study that I want to explore. First, I want to investigate the contextual background of wisdom in 1 Corinthians 1–4. Here, I will analyze the social situation affecting the life, ministry, and problems of the Corinthian church. In 1 Corinthians 1:26 Paul refers to people from different walks of life. Primarily though, many belong to the lower strata of the society. How might the mixed social composition of the church affect the unity and leadership of the church? How might the prevailing environment or culture affect the faith and conduct of the Corinthians in the church? In relation to this, I seek to establish to whom Paul is addressing 1 Corinthians 1–4. Is he writing to the church in general? Or is he writing to the influential members of the church who are allegedly causing the problems in the church? Second, I endeavor to find out the meaning of Paul's wisdom concept, in particular, "Christ, the wisdom of God" (1 Cor 1:24). Paul's discussion of his wisdom teaching is integrated in his discussion of the problems in the church. It seems Paul's response to the problems in the Corinthian church anchors on his understanding of true wisdom, that is, "Christ, the wisdom of God." Third, I will explore how Paul's wisdom teaching can provide a key for exploring how the three problems connect. Put another way, what is the significance of Paul's wisdom teaching in addressing the problems of the church? I establish how these problems fit together. I argue that Paul's wisdom teaching, particularly his discussion of "Christ, the wisdom of God" is his response to the problem of wisdom and the problems of division and boasting.

1.3 Methodology

In this study, I provide a sociological and rhetorical analysis of the text. I combine this with an exegesis of 1 Corinthians 1–4 seen against Paul's correspondence with the Corinthian church. Due to the different ways the text is approached from a sociological perspective, I rely on the approaches of Wayne Meeks, Gerd Theissen, and E. A. Judge, but adapt them for my purposes.[53] In the rhetorical analysis, I consider Paul's rhetoric in light of Greco-Roman rhetoric using the approach introduced by George A. Kennedy, in his book *New Testament Interpretation Through Rhetorical Criticism*, which was adapted by scholars including Duane Frederick Watson and Brian K. Peterson.[54]

---

53. Meeks, *First Urban Christians*; Theissen, *Social Setting*. This essay can also be found in Gerd Theissen, "The Sociological Interpretation of Religious Traditions: Its Methodological Problems as Exemplified in Early Christianity," in *The Bible and Liberation: Political and Social Hermeneutics*, ed. N. Gottwald (Maryknoll, NY: Orbis Books, 1984), 38–53; Judge, *Social Pattern*; Judge, "Early Christians," 4–15; Judge, "Early Christians: Part II," 125–37.

54. Kennedy, *New Testament Interpretation*; Watson, *Invention*; Peterson, *Eloquence*.

1.3.1 The Method of Sociological Interpretation

This section explains the method of sociological interpretation in the New Testament particularly in the Pauline Epistles.

1.3.1.1 The Sociological Approach of the New Testament

A Sociological approach has two major categories: social history and social-scientific method.[55] Social history focuses on the social description of the "social world" of early Christianity.[56] It explores its social world with the "acute concern for an accurate telling of 'social' conflicts, groups, and material culture."[57] Social description of early Christianity covers four topics. First, it describes social facts or *realia* such as their occupation and foodstuffs. Second, it describes the broader investigation into the "social and political history and theology."[58] Third, it describes the "*social organization* of early Christianity in terms of both the *social forces* which led to the rise of Christianity and the *social institutions* of early Christianity."[59] Fourth, it describes the social world of early Christianity "as the creation of a world of meaning which provided a plausibility structure for those who chose to inhabit it."[60] Three approaches are recommended here: (1) reconstruct what it meant or "felt like" to live during the time of the early Christians; (2) study how "man creates his world primarily through language"; (3) study how the environment affects the lives of the people with reference to the symbols and languages they used.[61]

The social-scientific method asserts that the effective way of bridging the cultural and historical gaps is to use anthropological, sociological, and social science models.[62] It explores the social and cultural systems of the ancient days to discover "meanings made possible and shaped by the social and cultural systems inhabited by both authors and intended audiences."[63] Bruce J.

---

55. Social-scientific criticism is also known as "social-scientific study of the Bible and the biblical world," "sociological exegesis," "sociological analysis," and "materialist reading" of the biblical material.

56. Martin, "Social-Scientific Criticism," 129.

57. Neyrey, "Social-Scientific Criticism," 178.

58. Smith, "Social Description," 19.

59. Smith, "Social Description," 20.

60. Smith, 21.

61. Smith, 21.

62. Martin, "Social-Scientific Criticism," 129.

63. Elliott, *What Is Social Scientific Criticism*, 8.

Malina shows the function of models in the interpretive process.[64] In this approach, the interpreter discerns the visual representations of the social setting and human behavior evoked by the text and appropriates a system of understanding with the use of modern categories, which are based on how the general social world works.[65] This representation is then used to analyze the beliefs, and social culture.

John Gager observes that both methods are involved in explaining social data but are distinct in their functions as social history focuses on social descriptions while social-scientific method builds on the foundations of social history.[66] As John H. Elliott explains, the historical-critical method (and social history) succeeded in collecting, identifying, and describing the social data but did not analyze it. Social-scientific criticism analyzes the meaning of the social data through the use of "questions and objectives, modes of analysis and processes of explanations" derived from social sciences.[67] Dale Martin does not see these methods as contrasting or distinct from each other. Rather, the issue centers on the use of "models," particularly what is a suitable model and how it is applied.[68]

The sociological approach has its own limitations and difficulties. The first limitation is the lack of sufficient sociological data available from the ancient world for research. Much of the data found in the New Testament are more theological than sociological in nature. Thus, analyses of early Christianity is limited.[69] Meeks alludes to this limitation as the reason why Christianity's "beginnings and earliest growth remain in many respects mysterious."[70]

A second limitation is the lack of agreement among scholars about the social context and identity of the first Christians. Judge challenges the popular view of Adolf Deissmann who claims that the first Christians belong to the lower class of the society by asserting that they were not altogether poor or

---

64. Malina, "Social Sciences," 229–42.
65. Malina, 232.
66. Gager, "Social Description," 429.
67. Elliott, *What Is Social Scientific Criticism*, 12–14.
68. Martin, "Social-Scientific Criticism," 129.
69. Scroggs, "Sociological Interpretation," 337–56. Cf. Gottwald, "Sociological Methods," 142–56.
70. Meeks, *First Urban Christians*, 1.

peasants but included patrons and household dependents.⁷¹ Gager calls them the "disprivileged" group, not only in reference to their economic status in the society but also in view of their tribal background.⁷² Thus, Malherbe implies a new consensus can be reached that though the first Christians may not belong to the upper level class of the society they were not composed also of the lowest bracket of the society.⁷³

1.3.1.2 Sociological Interpretation in Pauline Christianity

Sociological studies have given due focus to the fascinating references of social settings of the first century in Paul's letters. This section examines the works of Theissen, Meeks, and Judge in relation to the social environment of Pauline Christianity.

1.3.1.2.1 The Sociological Interpretation of Wayne Meeks

Meeks focuses on describing the social context of Pauline Christianity, that is, the world shared by the believers with other urban settlers, and their own social environment where they form their own patterns of interactions.⁷⁴ In particular, he studies the role and status of the first Christians.⁷⁵ He popularized the term "status inconsistency" or "status dissonance."⁷⁶ He argues that understanding people's status depends on the measure you use. That is, one's status cannot just be measured based on his economic status only because ancient society had various ways of ranking one's social status like family origin, occupation, etc. One could be rich and educated but if he does not come from a prestigious family, his social status and rank might still be affected. To assume that modern social stratification could easily fit as a model to measure ancient social status is a flawed approach. Thus, Meeks suggests several considerations in its study. First, "not all the dimensions have the same weight."⁷⁷ Education, profession, and economic capability have different values in social ranking. Second, "the weight of each dimension depends

---

71. Judge, *Social Pattern*, 60.
72. Gager, *Kingdom and Community*, 94–96.
73. Malherbe, *Social Aspects*, 31. Cf. Judge, "Social Identity," 118–27.
74. Meeks, *First Urban Christians*, 8.
75. Meeks, "Social Context," 266–77.
76. Meeks, 268.
77. Meeks, 268.

upon who is doing the weighing."[78] Personal perception of one's social rank could be different from others; perceptions of the upper class have more value than the common people. Third, "the 'fit' or correlation between different dimensions of status is itself an important measure of how one stands within one's society."[79] Ancient social ranking is multidimensional. So, Meeks studies how rankings are done in different levels. He analyzes their "ethnic origins, citizenship, personal liberty, wealth, and occupation" as well as the social context of these rankings; "for example, to be a freedman in the early years of Roman Corinth, a colony whose first settlers were mostly freedmen, would be less of a social liability than in Rome or in Antioch."[80]

1.3.1.2.2 The Sociological Interpretation of Gerd Theissen

Theissen's work covers the study of the roles, factors, and functions. The analysis of roles refers to the study of patterns of behavior. The analysis of factors refers to the study of how the social context influences the patterns of behavior. The analysis of function refers to the study of how the patterns of behavior affect its social context.[81]

The tension in studying the sociological aspect of the New Testament revolves around the problem of methodology, which is summed up in this question: How does one obtain information about sociological circumstances from religious expressions in our sources? Noting how the first Christian community, whose social origin was spawned in the rural areas of Palestine but rapidly grew in Hellenistic Mediterranean, was influencing society, Theissen asks, "How could this marginal, subcultural current conquer and transform an entire culture?" Since this is a sociological inquiry, Theissen clarifies that the study must focus on the community life, that is, how the members of the community interact with each other rather than on the individual life of its members. Attention must be given to the structural relationships as well as institutions in order to understand the interpersonal dynamics of the community life.[82]

---

78. Meeks, 268.
79. Meeks, 268.
80. Meeks, 268–69.
81. Theissen, *Sociology*, 3.
82. Theissen, *Social Setting*, 175–77.

Theissen recommends three approaches in his method: constructive, analytical, and comparative approaches. First, the constructive approach refers to the study of social data that describes the "social situation to which we owe the transmission and formulation of the texts."[83] It seeks to describe the different social groups as well as the identity of the first Christians (background, status, roles, etc.).[84] Under this approach, Theissen outlines three important problems: reliability, validity, and representativeness. The problem of reliability refers to whether the text that bears the social data was reliably transmitted and corroborated by scholars who have studied the same social data. It must also take into account the historical as well as the social identity of the source of the information. The problem of validity refers to the internal evidence that corroborates the historicity of the information. The problem of representativeness refers to whether the social data contain descriptions of social groups or institutions. Are there clues to show the existence of social groups or memberships?[85]

Second, in the analytical approach, inferences from events, norms, and symbols must be considered.[86] Inferences from events is the process of analyzing unusual data from historical events. This approach allows the interpreter to discover the background of the event or information, which is the "usual."[87] In addition, this approach studies "events which reoccur in relation to a particular feature," like Jesus's habit of visiting only the territories that belong to the cities but without actually entering them.[88] Finally, this approach studies conflicts that exist between groups and representatives of groups that usually reveal interesting social behavior, customs, and social assumptions.[89] Inferences from norms refers to the process of drawing insights from explicit norms (practical, ethical, judicial norms) or implicit regular social behaviors (speaking and literary activity). Practical norms have no sanctions for they operate based on shared convictions and beliefs, which also serve as the motivations of the members to act accordingly. Ethical and judicial norms

---

83. Theissen, 177.
84. Theissen, 177–78.
85. Theissen, 178–80.
86. Theissen, 180.
87. Theissen, 181.
88. Theissen, 181.
89. Theissen, 181–82.

usually have accompanying consequences that secure strict compliance by the members of the community.[90] Inferences from symbols refers to the process of analyzing life images used to communicate themes for life learning. In ecclesiological symbols, analysis involves the image and what it represents. Here, the representation of the image is defined while maintaining the reality of the image. For example, the body of Christ is used to refer to the members of the Christian community whose unity is portrayed by how the human body works together to accomplish an act.[91]

Third, comparative approach refers to the "procedure which considers texts which neither deal with, nor come from, early Christian groups."[92] This is the process of referring to non-Christian sources to look for clues that would corroborate the social data mentioned in the New Testament. Here, contemporary social groups and social situations are analyzed to help shed light on the data being studied. This procedure may focus either on identifying the contrasting features of non-biblical sources and Christianity or on establishing similar characteristics that Christianity shares with contemporary social groups, communities, organizations, or movements. The results may not be accurate but complementary enough to provide sufficient data for deeper investigation.[93]

1.3.1.2.3 The Sociological Interpretation of E. A. Judge

As a social historian, E. A. Judge's works are primarily devoted to studying the Pauline Christianity especially with reference to understanding Paul's rhetoric, Paul's relationship with the churches he has ministered, church structure, conflicts, and social classes.[94] His essays provide clearer definitions of the broader Greco-Roman context of the first Christian community and how it influences their social institutions.[95] His study in the Greco-Roman social *realia* includes "demographics, social classes, the structure of social

---

90. Theissen, 182–86.
91. Theissen, 187–91.
92. Theissen, 177.
93. Theissen, 192–95.
94. Scholer, *Social Distinctives*, xv.
95. Judge, *Social Pattern*, iii.

institutions, and cultural conventions related to social class (e.g. the uses of rhetoric)."[96]

In studying social institutions, Judge seeks to discover whether the first Christians represent a movement of lower classes or not. What is the social identity of the first Christians in relation to their broader social context? Is Christianity a movement of the underprivileged or not?[97] Second, Judge asserts that the greater concern is not the lack of resources but methodology. He points out that the appropriateness of using modern models to analyze the ancient social world is difficult to establish. He explains, "the failure to perceive this is hardly the fault of modern observers . . . The difficulty arises from the failure of the ancient observers to give an adequate account of their society. The Greek theory was indiscriminately applied throughout antiquity, in most cases obscuring the actual social organization."[98] Thus, Judge suggests that to be effective in this study, we must gain an adequate understanding of the identity of the first Christians, their purpose as a group, their activities, and their relationship to their social context.[99]

Noting early Christianity's rural origins yet urban development, Judge explains, "its writers are mainly Jews of Palestinian associations; their readers the Greek-speaking members of Hellenistic communities. It interprets the religious significance of certain events of Judaea to a public unfamiliar with that situation."[100] These writers intended their message to be explicable by the readers in their own Hellenistic context. Thus, we must seek to know the identity as well as the thinking patterns of the first Christians to discern how they could have understood it. We must learn to view things from their perspective if we are to understand how the writers intended it to be understood by them. Hence, Judge underscores identifying the meaning of the social data to its Hellenistic context as opposed to the tendency to prioritize its Hebraic origins. Judge explains, "the only meaning that can be certainly recovered from the Gospels in their present form is the meaning they were

---

96. Scholer, *Social Distinctives*, xv.
97. Judge, "Early Christians," 4–15
98. Judge, 5.
99. Judge, 8.
100. Judge, *Social Pattern*, 9.

intended to convey to their original readers. We must therefore begin with the readers and explain their social situation as it is shown in Acts and Epistles."[101]

1.3.1.3 Summary and Conclusion

Sociological interpretation of the New Testament ushers the interpreter into the social context where social interactions happen and social habits are practiced. Social history employs the principles of historical criticism in describing the social world while social-scientific method uses modern sociological and anthropological methods to analyze the social data. In principle, these methods are related. Their main difference is on the use of models. That is, identifying what is a suitable model and how it is applied. Social historians criticize the use of modern sociological models but social scientists claim that even social historians also use models; only they call it presuppositions, not models.

As a social historian, Meeks recognizes there are times theories might also aid the interpretive process. That is, one's primary objective is to provide the social description of first Christian community and, as needed, use models when the text requires it. Meeks is cautious in anachronistically using models due to the fact that there is no modern model that completely matches ancient society or can comprehensively analyze it. Meeks focuses his study in Pauline Christianity, that is, the role and status of the first Christians in view of their own social context. He asserts ancient society uses various ways of ranking the status of an individual. He calls this "status inconsistency" or "status dissonance." He argues that ranking in the society is not based solely on economic status but is also based on family origin, occupation, education, etc. Thus, in reference to the first Christians, no one should indiscriminately assume that just because they belong to the lower class of the society, they were poor people or slaves.

Theissen's sociological study involves the study of roles (patterns of behavior), factors (social context's influences on patterns of behavior), functions (patterns of behavior's effect on its social context) of the first Christian community. Patterned after form critical method, he explores the text using the constructive method (the social situation that breeds the formulation as well as the transmission of the text), analytical method (learning from events,

---

101. Judge, 9–10.

norms, and symbols), and comparative method (referring to non-Christian sources to look for clues that would corroborate the social data mentioned in the New Testament).

Judge's essays are aimed at explaining the Pauline Christianity in view of its Greco-Roman context. He focuses on studying their social *realia* specifically understanding their social identity (social status, rankings, and rhetoric) and how their social context influences them. Judge observes that the writers want to make the message comprehensible to the readers so he uses terms understandable to them in their own context. Thus, he asserts the importance of studying the readers so we would know their thinking as well as reasoning processes if we are to understand the intended meaning of the writer, that is, how he intended it to be understood by his readers. We must think as they think and interpret the passage according to how the readers might have interpreted it.

How does this research propose to proceed in the sociological interpretation of the New Testament? Still the text is the best place to begin in our sociological research. The primary objective is to explore the social world of the first Christian community and use theories when the text requires it. The goal of the study is to allow the text to direct the interpretive process.

Sociological interpretation of the New Testament must be approached with a broader perspective especially in establishing the identity and social context of the first Christians. Thus, we must allow for a more comprehensive way of measuring one's ranking in the society, not only basing it on their economic capacity but looking at how all these factors (economic, education, family origins, occupation, etc.) affect individual status in society. Then, in addition, we must study the roles (patterns of behavior), factors (social context's influences to patterns of behavior), and functions (patterns of behavior's effect to its social context) of the first Christian community. This is where constructive, analytical, and comparative methods come into place. Every social detail has to be tested to attest its historical validity to strengthen the quality of the research.

Finally, we must approach the text with the perspective of the first readers. That is, we must seek to understand how they think, how they see things, and how they listen or read to enable us to think, see, hear, or read the message the way they did it when they first encountered it. It allows us to reconstruct not only the dynamics of the first Christian community's interaction but more importantly to perceive and receive the message as it was intended when it was first written.

1.3.2 The Rhetorical Method

This section discusses how rhetorical criticism developed and explains the method.

1.3.2.1 Development of Rhetorical Criticism in the New Testament

Among the early proponents of rhetorical analysis in the Bible were Augustine of Hippo, the reformers, Johannes Weiss, and his students Rudolf Bultmann and Hans Windisch.[102] Towards the end of the nineteenth century the practice of rhetorical criticism declined due to some objections from scholars like Eduard Norden. Norden criticized Carl Friedrich George Heinrici's rhetorical analysis of 2 Corinthians because it did not meet the standards of classical rhetoric. Later, Norden retracted his earlier criticism after Heinrici responded to him. Norden's retraction though failed to influence other scholars who initially agreed with him. Those who persisted in their objections of rhetorical analysis even reduced it to mere style. Thus, rhetorical analysis continues to decline especially when schools started to remove rhetoric from their curricula. In addition, interest in other topics like apocalyptic, myth, and rituals shifted the focus of New Testament scholarship.[103] Towards the end of 1960s a renewed interest in rhetorical analysis began to surface. The works of Amos Wilder and Robert Funk helped spark the revival of the rhetorical analysis of the Scriptures. Wilder, who is widely acclaimed as the father of rhetorical analysis, argues the rhetorical features of the text "reveal the social-historical setting and exigence which produced them."[104] Funk also asserts Paul's letters must be interpreted using rhetorical analysis because it essentially bears the evidence of oral expressions as obviously found in the dialogues, arguments, and other forms of human verbal interactions. Funk admits that the greater challenge in analyzing the rhetoric of Paul is not in understanding the written text but in listening to the rhetorical voices enunciated by the written text.[105]

---

102. Watson and Hauser, *Rhetorical Criticism*, 101–9.
103. Peterson, *Eloquence*, 9–11.
104. Watson and Hauser, *Rhetorical Criticism*, 106–7.
105. Funk, *Language*, 248–49.

In 1968, James Muilenburg picked up the discussion. During his presidential address at the annual meeting of Society of Biblical Literature, he challenged the scholars to move beyond form criticism and explore the value of rhetorical criticism in the interpretation of Scripture.[106] Muilenburg asserts that the text must be "read and heard precisely as it is spoken."[107] It is essential to explore the creative literary features of the text because "a responsible and proper articulation of the words in their linguistic patterns and in their precise formulations will reveal to us the texture and fabric of the writer's thought, not only what it is that he thinks, but as he thinks it."[108] There are two important concerns of rhetorical criticism. First, the interpreter determines (the beginning and the end of) the rhetorical unit and analyzes how the major theme or exigency is resolved. Second, the interpreter identifies the structure of the rhetorical unit and the rhetorical devices being used by the author such as parallelism, strophes, meters, rhetorical questions, and repetitions.[109] Scholars took his challenge and used it to interpret Old Testament passages.

On the other hand, following the earlier works of Wilder and Funk, New Testament scholarship took a renewed interest in rhetorical analysis. Judge, one of the early revivalists, notes the challenge in defining the rhetoric of Paul in his letters.[110] He suggests Paul may have not been trained formally in ancient rhetoric but he exhibits an unconventional style of rhetoric that invites further attention. Noting the assessment of John Chrysostom on Paul's work, Judge writes "Paul was simply no kind of expert but that his power of speech would still be the marvel of all men until the end of time because in knowledge and penetration of thought he was, in contrast, no layman."[111] It is in this context he calls for an exploration and "complete analysis of the New Testament rhetoric."[112]

Hans Betz's article, "The Literary Composition and Function of Paul's Letter to the Galatians," is the one of the first major attempts to use rhetorical

---

106. Muilenburg, "Form Criticism and Beyond," 1–18.
107. Muilenburg, 5.
108. Muilenburg, 7.
109. Muilenburg, 5–17.
110. Judge, "Paul's Boasting," 37–50.
111. Judge, 41.
112. Judge, 45.

analysis in the New Testament.[113] In his article he argues that ancient Greco-Roman rhetoric can be used to analyze the rhetorical features of Galatians. Despite receiving strong criticisms for his work on Galatians, Betz succeeded in providing a working analysis of its invention and arrangement of arguments using Greco-Roman rhetoric and epistolography.[114]

In 1984, George A. Kennedy fills this gap with his book *New Testament Interpretation Through Rhetorical Criticism*. In this book, Kennedy outlines five steps towards a methodological analysis using rhetorical criticism. After dealing with some basic methodological issues regarding rhetorical criticism, I will look at each of the five steps in order.

1.3.2.2 The Method of Rhetorical Criticism

Like Muilenburg, Kennedy sees rhetorical criticism as a complementary method to form, redaction, historical, and literary criticisms. He defines rhetoric as that "quality in discourse by which a speaker or writer seeks to accomplish his purposes."[115] Aristotle considers rhetoric as a means of persuading people, not for personal gain or interest, but towards what is right and just. It is used to challenge as well as refute the unfair use of arguments (i.e. false arguments).[116] Kennedy explains that in rhetorical criticism, the speaker/writer seeks to persuade their audience through a carefully crafted argument based on reason and evidence to respond to the message they convey. In similar manner, the New Testament books are written to convince the readers to act upon the message the writers intend to convey. Thus, these works bear rhetorical elements and must be analyzed rhetorically. In rhetorical criticism, the text is analyzed in its final form with the goal of understanding the intent of the author or the editor as well as how the target readers may understand or receive it. Kennedy suggests the Bible must be analyzed rhetorically "as it would be read by an early Christian, by an inhabitant of the Greek-speaking world in which rhetoric was the core subject of formal education and in

---

113. Betz, "Literary Composition," 353–79. His subsequent commentary in Galatians demonstrates his expanded work in analyzing Galatians using Graeco-Roman rhetoric and epistolography.

114. Betz, "Literary Composition," 353–54.

115. Kennedy, *New Testament Interpretation*, 3.

116. Aristotle, *Rhet.* 1.1.1355a.12.

which even those without formal education necessarily developed cultural preconceptions about appropriate discourse."[117]

Watson traces the roots of New Testament rhetoric to at least three sources: "Jewish heritage, that heritage independent and dependent upon Graeco-Roman rhetoric, and more directly from Graeco-Roman rhetoric itself." Thus, he equally pushes for the historical reading of Paul's letters using Greco-Roman rhetoric. Since Paul and his readers are familiar with ancient rhetoric it is possible to discern how the author would have wanted his readers to understand his letter and how the readers would have perceived the message of Paul. Watson explains that this approach "uses a systematized and well-conceptualized discipline from the Greco-Roman era to analyze the New Testament . . . It enables the interpreter to hear and respond to the text in a fashion akin to the original first century audience."[118] On the other hand, Peterson points out the relationship of rhetorical criticism to social history. He explains, "Rhetoric treats a speech as a social event, as an attempt to re-shape the social realities which it addresses. Ancient rhetoricians emphasized that a speech could never be separated from its situation."[119] That gaining an adequate reading of the persuasiveness of the argument can be deduced by studying its social situation.[120] Judge underscores Paul's arguments are not only aimed at addressing the issues he felt compelled to respond but also the social situation of his readers who may have influenced the exigencies he was dealing at that time. Judge writes,

> Of one thing we may be sure, that such is the subtlety of the lost rhetorical art, that until we have it back under control we can hardly think we know how to read passages which both by style and belong to Paul's struggle with rhetorically trained opponents for the support of his rhetorically fastidious converts.[121]

Jeffrey T. Reed sought to establish the relationship of Paul's letters to ancient Greco-Roman rhetoric.[122] He answered these questions: "Did he employ

---

117. Kennedy, *New Testament Interpretation*, 3–5.
118. Watson and Hauser, *Rhetorical Criticism*, 109–10.
119. Peterson, *Eloquence*, 14.
120. Peterson, 14.
121. Judge, "Paul's Boasting," 47–48.
122. Reed, "Using Ancient Rhetorical Categories," 292–324.

the categories of the ancient rhetorical handbooks, especially those of his day? That is, when Paul attempted to persuade the recipients of his letters, did he form his arguments from the perspective of contemporary rhetorical practices?"[123]

Reed observes the presence of invention, style, and arrangement in Paul's letters as well as the basic characteristics of species of ancient rhetoric: judicial, deliberative, and epideictic speeches. Although these species are primarily used in oral speeches but ancient practices show that people have adapted these species in writing letters to people in distant places to pass important information. There is no explicit indicator though that these letters were written under the same circumstances of oral speeches. For example, a judicial speech's location is the courtroom. A letter may bear a judicial-like tone but it is not composed within the setting of the courtroom. In the same manner, in his letters, particularly in 1 Corinthians, Paul addresses issues that determine innocence or guilt as well as whether such actions or decisions are beneficial to the greater community. His letters also contain praise and blame but none of these can be classified as judicial, deliberative, or epideictic in its pure form because his letters are written with different contexts from the oral speeches. The letters resemble the function but not the exact form.[124] Though Paul's letter employs the basic discipline of argumentation, "it is doubtful that he addressed his assemblies with the precise rhetoric of the lawyer, or the exact speech of a politician, or the identical style of the public orator."[125]

Paul's letters resemble elements of ancient Greco-Roman rhetoric but the parallel is indirect. It is likely because this method is common in his day. Also, Paul's letters are written for different contexts and purposes. Thus, it is difficult to establish Paul's dependence on ancient rhetorical method because the "similarity is functional, not formal."[126] Matthew R. Malcolm affirms this view citing the lack of reliable evidence to establish Paul's dependence on ancient rhetorical formal conventions.[127] Kennedy upholds Paul may have not studied Greek rhetoric formally but its extensive practice may have influenced him.[128]

---

123. Reed, 295.
124. Reed, 296–301.
125. Reed, 314.
126. Reed, 308.
127. Matthew, *Paul and the Rhetoric*, 70.
128. Kennedy, *New Testament Interpretation*, 10–11.

Reed recognizes the benefits of analyzing Paul's letters using Greco-Roman rhetoric but he urges the interpreter to use it with caution. That is, the safest approach to analyze Paul's method of argumentation is to describe it only, not prescribe. It is possible that some of Paul's letters may not strictly follow the pattern of Greco-Roman rhetoric or contain all its elements. In this case, the interpreter must limit their analysis to the elements present in the text and let the text guide the direction of the analysis.[129] Thus, using ancient rhetorical method in interpreting Paul's letter must be carried with "methodological prudence" as the similarities are functional rather than formal.[130] Kennedy also affirms that describing logical and structural features of Paul's letters using ancient rhetorical theory allows the interpreter to gain better appreciation of the meaning of the text.[131]

The five steps are: (1) determine the rhetorical unit, (2) analyze the rhetorical situation, (3) determine the species of rhetoric and the stasis theory, (4) analyze invention, arrangement, and style, (5) evaluate rhetorical effectiveness.

1.3.2.2.1 The Rhetorical Unit

The first step is to determine the rhetorical unit. A rhetorical unit is a persuasive or argumentative unit that calls the reader to respond to subject matters that can be disturbing, challenging, or affirming.[132] A rhetorical unit can be a main or a sub-rhetorical unit and it has an opening, middle, and closing section. A speech can be a sub-rhetorical unit when it is found within a larger scope of material such as a book.[133] If a sub-rhetorical unit is detected it might contain an *inclusio*, which must be interpreted in relation to the main rhetorical unit. The task is to determine the relationships and functions of these units to one another.[134]

---

129. Reed, "Using Ancient Rhetorical Categories," 314.
130. Reed, 322.
131. Kennedy, *New Testament Interpretation*, 12.
132. Wuellner, "Where is Literary Criticism," 448–63.
133. Kennedy, *New Testament Interpretation*, 33. Wuellner adds that other sub-rhetorical units are "metaphors and parables, sentential sayings and apophthegms, macarisms and hymns, commandments and parénesis, etc." See Wuellner, "Where is Literary Criticism," 448–63.
134. Kennedy, *New Testament Interpretation*, 33–34.

1.3.2.2.2 The Rhetorical Situation

The second step analyzes the rhetorical situation. Lloyd F. Bitzer introduces this concept in his article, "The Rhetorical Situation."[135] Bitzer defines the rhetorical situation as the "complex of persons, events, objects, and relations presenting an actual or potential exigence which can be completely or partially removed if discourse, introduced into the situation, can so constrain human decision or action as to bring about the significant modification of the exigence."[136] Ernst R. Wendland clarifies that the primary objective of the discourse is to "modify (i.e., reinforce or change) the cognitive, emotive, and/or volitional stance of the intended audience."[137] Rhetorical discourse takes place because a rhetorical situation compels the writer to respond to it. This rhetorical situation provides the context by which the rhetorical discourse is created.

Bitzer presents several points of consideration in understanding the rhetorical situation. First, not every response to a situation is considered a rhetorical act. A response is considered a rhetorical act when the rhetorical situation actually happened, not imaginary, fictitious, adapted, or created. Second, a rhetorical act as a fitting response implies that the author understands the rhetorical situation. It is imperative that the rhetor possesses an accurate assessment of the rhetorical situation in order for them to provide a fitting response. If the response does not fit the situation then it "missed the mark."[138] Brinton suggests that a fitting response does not only indicate an appropriate rhetorical response but also appropriate prescribed actions that must be carried out by the audience in order to modify the situation.[139] Certain difficulty might be encountered in the assessment of the rhetorical situation especially when it is perceived differently by the rhetor and the audience or by other parties informed about the rhetorical situation. It is essential, then, that the rhetor understands the facts and their biases and interests. They must rectify not only the aspects that may affect the audience but also the ones that may affect them.[140] Third, Bitzer notes the rhetorical

---

135. Bitzer, "Rhetorical Situation," 1–14.
136. Bitzer, 4.
137. Wendland, "Aspects of Rhetorical Analysis," 169–96.
138. Bitzer, "Rhetorical Situation," 9–11.
139. Brinton, "Situation in the Theory," 234–48.
140. Brinton, 243–44.

situation may have simple or complex structure. A simple structure has only one exigency, a definite audience, and one identified constraint. A complex structure has more than one element involved in the rhetorical situation. Finally, rhetorical situations may also persist or evolve.[141]

A rhetorical situation has three components: exigency, audience, and constraints. Bitzer defines exigency as "an imperfection marked by urgency; it is a defect, an obstacle, something waiting to be done, a thing which is other than it should be."[142] Bitzer notes it is possible to find many exigencies in one rhetorical unit but they may not be all rhetorical exigencies. An exigency is rhetorical when it can be modified through a rhetorical response. If an exigency is not modifiable, like death, or if it can be modified by other means other than rhetorical discourse, then it is not a rhetorical exigency. A rhetorical unit has "at least one controlling exigence which functions as the organizing principle: it specifies the audience to be addressed and the change to be effected."[143]

A rhetorical audience refers to the persons to whom the discourse is directed and who are expected to respond or mediate the change that the discourse requires.[144] Constraints refer to "persons, events, objects, and relations which are parts of the situation because they have the power to constrain decision and action needed to modify the exigence."[145] It may include "beliefs, attitudes, documents, facts, traditions, images, interests, motives and the like."[146]

1.3.2.2.3 The Species of Rhetoric and Stasis Theory

In the third step we determine the species of rhetoric and the stasis theory. There are three species of rhetoric: judicial, deliberative, and epideictic. Judicial (or forensic) involves accusations and defense where the rhetor seeks "to persuade the audience to make judgments about events occurring in the past."[147] Here, in cases where some wrongdoings are committed, the rhetor seeks to establish both the "frame of mind of the wrongdoer" as well as motive

---

141. Bitzer, "Rhetorical Situation," 11–13.
142. Bitzer, 6.
143. Bitzer, 6–7.
144. Bitzer, 7–8.
145. Bitzer, 8.
146. Bitzer, 8.
147. Kennedy, *New Testament Interpretation*, 19.

of the wrongdoing whether it is based on voluntary actions (habit, reason, anger, or desire) or involuntary actions (chance, nature, or compulsion).[148] Deliberative rhetoric involves giving advice, persuasion, and dissuasion on matters that may be beneficial or harmful to the audience in the future.[149] The time referent of deliberative rhetoric is usually the immediate future.[150] Though there are situations when it may deal with matters at the present time.[151] Deliberative rhetoric tackles matters that can be modified within the control or ability of the audience like war and peace, legislation, and defense of the country.[152] Epideictic rhetoric refers to the giving of praise or blame in public speeches to persuade the audience to "hold or reaffirm some point of view in the present, as when he celebrates or denounces some person or some quality."[153] Here, the rhetor establishes who is the "noble or disgraceful."[154]

It is possible to find all three species in one rhetorical unit but there is always a major species that runs through the entire argument.[155] The letters of Paul "are typically not a single rhetorical species, but rather a mix of species."[156] Quintilian observes how in some cases deliberative and epideictic rhetoric complement each other in a single rhetorical unit because where deliberative advises or admonishes, epideictic praises or blames.[157] The interpreter must be careful to avoid the tendency to categorize an entire Pauline letter into one species because in Pauline letters the rhetorical situation can change from one rhetorical unit to another as in the case of 1 Corinthians.[158] Reed echoes a similar warning over the danger of a sweeping categorization of Paul's letter into one species.[159]

Stasis theory "is the system for determining the basic definite question at issue in a case when it may be obscure or when numerous questions may be

---

148. Aristotle, *Rhet.* 1.10.1368.
149. Watson, *Invention*, 10.
150. Kennedy, *New Testament Interpretation*, 36.
151. Aristotle, *Rhet.* 1.8.1366.
152. Aristotle, *Rhet.* 1.4.1359–1.4.1360.
153. Kennedy, *New Testament Interpretation*, 19.
154. Aristotle, *Rhet.* 1.3.1358.
155. Kennedy, *New Testament Interpretation*, 19.
156. Watson, "Three Species of Rhetoric," 42.
157. Quintilian, *Inst.* 3.7.28.
158. Watson, "Three Species of Rhetoric," 42.
159. Reed, "Using Ancient Rhetorical Categories," 314.

present."¹⁶⁰ It is the basis of the arguments being "waged."¹⁶¹ Cicero asserts that in every case or matter being disputed, the questions revolve around these four kinds of stasis: fact, definition, quality, and jurisdiction (objection).¹⁶² In the stasis of fact, the objective is to determine whether a thing has happened, or is happening, or has been done by a person being accused. In stasis of definition, the facts are already admitted but "the meanings of particular terms" are still to be defined or are being questioned. In stasis of quality, the act is admitted but whether the act is justifiable or not remains to be determined.¹⁶³ In the stasis of jurisdiction (objection), "the legitimacy of the particular legal action is questioned."¹⁶⁴ Although these four kinds of stasis are applicable to all kinds of species, they are oftentimes more applicable to judicial speeches.¹⁶⁵

1.3.2.2.4 Invention, Arrangement, and Style

The fourth step analyzes invention, arrangement, and style.¹⁶⁶ Invention deals with finding concrete arguments that establish the probability of the case being presented.¹⁶⁷ It refers to the composition of arguments based on external and internal proofs. External proof is a proof not developed by the author but includes witnesses and documents. In the New Testament, common external proofs are "quotations of Scripture, the evidence of miracles, and the naming of witnesses."¹⁶⁸ Internal proof is developed by the author based on propositions that include argumentation by *ethos* (ethical), *pathos* (pathetical), and *logos* (logical).¹⁶⁹

Ethos refers to "moral character and conduct . . . as a means of artificial proof, the rhetor seeks to show his own and his client's *ethos* in the best light and his opponent's in the worst."¹⁷⁰ In deliberative speeches, the speaker must demonstrate their authority based on their wisdom and character so that their

---

160. Watson, *Invention*, 12.
161. Peterson, *Eloquence*, 24.
162. Cicero, *De or.* 2.25.105–109.
163. Peterson, *Eloquence*, 24.
164. Peterson, 307–13.
165. Watson, *Invention*, 13.
166. Watson, 13.
167. Cicero, *Inv.* 1.7.9.
168. Kennedy, *New Testament Interpretation*, 14.
169. Watson, *Invention*, 14.
170. Watson, 14–15.

audience can trust their judgments regarding what is beneficial or harmful to the audience.[171] *Pathos* refers to the method used to arouse the emotions among the audience "with the purpose of eliciting a favorable response to the speaker's words."[172] Some examples of *pathos* are "astonishment, irony, sarcasm, threat, promise, affection, wise counsel, and Christian concern."[173] *Logos* has two kinds of reasoning, induction (example) and deduction (enthymeme or rhetorical syllogism).[174]

Induction (example) refers to the process of asking questions using argument by analogy (questions that build on each other) in order to lead the one being asked to agree with the view or action proposed by the one asking the questions. The objective is to bring the one being asked to a point where they concede to the logical conclusion implied by the questions.[175] Induction involves citing past events in order to draw insights that might be relevant to the actions required at present.[176] Deduction (enthymeme or rhetorical syllogism) refers to the "form of argument which draws a probable conclusion from the fact under consideration itself, when this probable conclusion is set forth and recognized by itself it proves itself by its own import and reasoning."[177] Aristotle suggests induction is more appropriate for deliberative rhetoric, deduction for judicial rhetoric, and since there is no dispute involved in epideictic rhetoric, amplification is more suitable to it.[178] Richard N. Longenecker notes that "whereas enthymeme argues from a premise to a conclusion or vice versa, argument by example seeks to persuade by appealing to a specific person, thing, or situation to establish or illustrate a general concept, principle or truth."[179] Aristotle highlights the supreme value of having a high degree of competence in logical reasoning in the study of

---

171. Quintilian, *Inst.* 3.8.13.
172. Longenecker, *Galatians*, cxviii.
173. Longenecker, cxviii.
174. Cicero, *Inv.* 1.31.51; Aristotle, *Rhet.* 1.2.1356b.8. This is a rhetorical description of reasoning, not logical description. Aristotle calls *example* a *rhetorical induction* and *enthymeme* a *rhetorical syllogism*. Cicero prefers to use *induction* for the term *example* and *deduction* for the term *enthymeme* or *rhetorical syllogism*.
175. Cicero, *Inv.* 1.31.51–54.
176. Aristotle, *Rhet.* 2.20.1393.
177. Cicero, *Inv.* 1.34.57.
178. Aristotle, *Rhet.* 1.9.1368.
179. Longenecker, *Galatians*, cxvi.

character and virtues. It is also essential to have a good grasp of the nature, origins, and manner of emotions so that one can successfully generate it from their audience.[180] Some examples of *logos* are enthymeme, argument by definition, argument by dissociation of ideas, argument by the severance of a group and its members, means-end argument, argument by repetition, and amplification.[181]

Arrangement refers to the structure of the rhetorical unit. These are *exordium, narratio, partitio* or *propositio, probatio* (*probatio* also may include *refutatio*), and *peroratio*.[182] *Exordium* is the introductory statement of the author and aimed at preparing the audience to be attentive, open, well-disposed, and engaged for the rest of the speech.[183] *Exordium* is the part where the speaker begins to appeal to the emotions of the audience.[184] This is where the speaker engages with the audience to excite them as well as disarm their objections, prejudices, or biases towards the topic being presented. In epideictic speech, the speaker must be able to convince their audience that their speech expresses their own convictions and perspective of the subject matter being tackled. That is, if they are giving praise, the audience must perceive that it is sincere as well as authentic and not just meaningless platitudes.[185] Cicero notes that in order to increase the level of success in preparing their audience to accept their speech, the speaker must prepare a good *exordium* by understanding well the nature of the case they are going to address to the crowd.[186]

There are five kinds of cases in *exordium*: honorable, difficult, mean, ambiguous, and obscure. Honorable cases refer to matters generally accepted as deserving to be defended or attacked. Difficult cases refer to matters that have "alienated the sympathy of those who are about to listen to the speech."[187] Mean cases refer to matters the audience deem trivial and "unworthy of serious attention."[188] Ambiguous cases refer to matters where reaching a de-

---

180. Aristotle, *Rhet.* 1.2.1356.
181. Longenecker, *Galatians*, cxv–cxviii.
182. Witherington, *Conflict and Community*, 44.
183. Quintilian, *Inst.* 4.1.5; Peterson, *Eloquence*, 24.
184. Quintilian, *Inst.* 3.8.12.
185. Aristotle, *Rhet.* 3.14.1415.
186. Cicero, *Inv.* 1.15.20.
187. Cicero, *Inv.* 1.15.20.
188. Cicero, *Inv.* 1.15.20.

cision is doubtful because the nature of the case is "partly honourable and partly discreditable."[189] Obscure cases refer to matters which are complex and difficult to comprehend.[190] Deliberative speeches, however, do not usually require an *exordium* because oftentimes the audience is familiar with the subject matter already. They usually request the topic to be discussed. There are cases though that an *exordium* is necessary for the benefit of the speaker or when the audience or recipients are not aware of or concerned about the seriousness of the exigency especially its harmful effect upon them.[191]

Narratio (or statement of facts) refers to the "persuasive exposition of that which either has been done or is supposed to have been done."[192] It refers to the presentation of the nature of the subject matter which must be decided upon.[193] *Narratio* also consists of statements indicating the reasons or motives of the inquiry.[194] *Partitio* (or *propositio*) refers to presentation of the propositions the author wants to prove. It may also contain the proposition of the opponent.[195] *Partitio* also refers to the author's main thesis and advice. Usually, deliberative rhetoric does not have *narratio* but the author may include it after the *propositio*.[196] *Probatio* refers to the presentation of proof to prove the case of the author against their audience. In deliberative rhetoric, a *probatio* states the reasons for the readers to follow "the course of action that is being advised" with a vision of how their obedience would benefit them in the future.[197] It may also include *refutatio*. *Refutatio* refers to the part where the arguments of the opponent or the audience (especially if the some of the people in the audience are part of the exigency) are weakened or refuted through the following ways: "Either one or more of its assumptions are not granted, or if the assumptions are granted it is denied that a conclusion follows

---

189. Cicero, *Inv.* 1.15.20.
190. Cicero, *Inv.* 1.15.20.
191. Aristotle, *Rhet.* 3.14.1415; Quintilian, *Inst.* 3.8.6.
192. Quintilian, *Inst.* 4.2.31.
193. Witherington, *Conflict and Community*, 44; Quintilian, *Inst.* 4.2.1.
194. Quintilian, *Inst.* 4.2.52.
195. Watson, *Invention*, 21.
196. Kennedy, *New Testament Interpretation*, 24.
197. Witherington, *Conflict and Community*, 106.

from them, or the form of the argument is shown to be fallacious, or a strong argument is met by one equally strong or stronger."[198]

Peroratio is the final emotional summary appeal in view of the *probatio*, where the author seeks to "arouse the audience's emotions in favor of the speaker's viewpoint by amplifying what has been said before."[199] *Peroratio* has three parts: summing up, *indignatio*, and *conquestio*. Summing up refers to the process of gathering and collating all the arguments into one concise paragraph in order to give the audience a collective idea of the arguments at one glance.[200] *Indignatio* refers to the process of "exciting indignation or ill-will against the opponent."[201] The presentation centers on certain topics to highlight how such actions, if permitted, could potentially influence or destroy the lives of many people including those in authority. In view of the gravity of the problem, the speaker calls for the urgency of preventing the destructive or dreaded effect it may bring to the greater community of people. It may also involve an appeal to pass judgment on the guilty party immediately to alter the current situation to avoid any further damage to the weak and innocent like children and women.[202] In the *conquestio*, the goal is to appeal to the gentle spirit of the audience to gain sympathy so they will be moved to act accordingly. To accomplish this, the speaker explains to the audience the destructive effect of the exigency to their children, love ones, current state of peace, unity, and prosperity if the exigency is permitted to exist.[203]

Style refers to the manner of presentation of arguments in order to achieve the desired persuasiveness of the speech.[204] It has four virtues: correctness, clarity, ornamentation, and propriety. Correctness refers to grammar. Clarity refers to how the ideas are arranged to make it more persuasive.[205] Aristotle cautions that the lack of clarity obscures the meaning of the speech. It renders the speech powerless in persuading the audience.[206] Ornamentation includes

---

198. Cicero, *Inv.* 1.42.79.
199. Witherington, *Conflict and Community*, 44.
200. Cicero, *Inv.* 1.52.98–100.
201. Cicero, *Inv.* 1.52.98.
202. Cicero, *Inv.* 1.53.100–54.105.
203. Cicero, *Inv.* 1.55.106–09.
204. Aristotle, *Rhet.* 3.1.1403.
205. Kennedy, *New Testament Interpretation*, 25.
206. Aristotle, *Rhet.* 3.2.1404.

the use of figures of speech in order to emphasize ideas. Propriety refers to how the speaker matches their style with their content.[207] The speaker's style must display the emotions evoked by the content of their speech. That is, they must be able to express indignation when talking about injustices or wrongdoings, admiration when praising good deeds or things, compassion as well as grief when lamenting over death or losses, and other situations that require appropriate expressions.[208] Propriety also refers to the proficiency of the speaker in using the right terms to identify things. The speaker must carefully choose words that are not obscene but decent and truthful as well as intelligible to the audience.[209] Style uses figures of speech and thought such as anaphora, antithesis, and rhetorical question.[210]

Watson notes that amplification is another helpful aspect of the study that is closely related to invention, arrangement, and style. Amplification refers to the method of arguing to convince the audience by "arousing emotion" like instigating anger or appealing for compassion. The use of amplification varies depending on the purpose. If the purpose is exhortation, it points out the good and bad things. Amplification is usually used to amplify the arguments at the *peroratio* especially after presenting the proof (*refutatio*). Some of the methods of amplification are the use of strong words (synonyms, exaggeration, metaphor), comparison, and repetition.[211]

1.3.2.2.5 Evaluating Rhetorical Effectiveness

The fifth step evaluates rhetorical effectiveness. Here, the interpreter evaluates the overall effectiveness of the rhetorical unit in addressing the issues discussed. It evaluates whether the rhetoric has effectively addressed the exigency that it seeks to modify. The interpreter seeks also to analyze the rhetoric's impact on the audience. Is the audience convinced or moved to act towards the desired results or changes as urged in the rhetoric?[212] The

---

207. Kennedy, *New Testament Interpretation*, 25.
208. Aristotle, *Rhet.* 3.7.1408.
209. Quintilian, *Inst.* 4.2.1.
210. Kennedy, *New Testament Interpretation*, 25–26.
211. Watson, *Invention*, 26–28.
212. Watson, *Invention*, 28.

interpreter seeks to answer the question, "is the detailed analysis consistent with the overall impact of the rhetorical unit?"[213]

1.4 Overview of the Study and Application of the Method to the Study

Chapter 1 is the introduction of the study. It provides a brief definition of the problems of division, boasting, and wisdom. Also, it explains the assumptions and limitations as well as the significance of the study. In addition, it explores the state of the question and explains the research problem. Further, it discusses the methodology and provides an overview of the study and the application of the method to the study.

Chapter 2 considers the sociological interpretation of 1 Corinthians 1–4. It analyzes the events affecting the life and ministry of the Corinthian church in view of the problems the Corinthian church is facing. It explores how the social background of the members of the Corinthian church may have contributed to the problems in the church. Also, it explores the probable connection between the problems of division, boasting, and wisdom.

Chapter 3 provides a rhetorical analysis of 1 Corinthians 1–4. This analysis provides an integrated discussion of the meaning of Paul's wisdom concept and the nature of the Corinthian problems since Paul's discussion of his wisdom concept is integrated in his discussion of the problems of division, boasting and wisdom. It explores further how the problems are related.

Chapter 4 analyzes and assesses how Paul uses his wisdom teaching to address the problems of division, boasting, and wisdom. It establishes how these problems fit together and Paul's wisdom teaching, particularly his discussion on "Christ, the wisdom of God" as his response not only to the problem of wisdom but also to the problems of division and boasting.

Chapter 5 is the conclusion of the study. It also highlights the contribution of the study to the Pauline study particularly in 1 Corinthians 1–4. It also notes some possible areas of further research in view of the results of the study.

---

213. Kennedy, *New Testament Interpretation*, 38.

CHAPTER 2

The Social Context of the Corinthian Church

This chapter investigates the social background of wisdom in 1 Corinthians 1–4. In particular, I explore the social context of the Corinthian church. Social context refers to the political, economic, familial, educational, and religious life of the people where meaningful interactions take place based on shared beliefs and practices.[1] In view of this, I explore the ethnic composition of Roman Corinth, social status, patronage, and first-century sophistic practice to find possible connections for how the social context may have influenced the conduct of the Corinthian believers among themselves.

Further, this chapter demonstrates how the social background of the Corinthian believers may shed light on the influences that gave rise to the problems of division, boasting, and wisdom. This chapter also explores how these three problems are connected.

2.1 The Social Profile of Roman Corinth

When Lucius Mummius conquered Corinth in 146 BC. many residents fled the city but those who remained were either killed or sold into slavery especially the women and children.[2] Mummius looted the city and burned the buildings.[3] Many of the buildings (mostly built of stones) survived the fire

---

1. Meeks, *First Urban Christians*, 8.
2. Engels, *Roman Corinth*, 8–15. Cf. Fotopoulos, "1 Corinthians," 413–33.
3. Strabo, *Geogr.* 8.6.23.

though.[4] Nancy Bookidis asserts that recent excavations show less evidence that the alleged destruction of Corinth was total. Walls were breached but many buildings were hardly damaged especially the Sanctuary of Demeter and Kore.[5]

Just before his death Julius Caesar began to rebuild Corinth as a Roman colony in 44 BC. Some of the buildings that had survived were restored and given a Roman architectural look.[6] The city was given a Latin name, *Colonia Laus Iulia Corinthiensis* and around 12,000–16,000 colonists came as settlers.[7] Most of the new settlers who came from Rome were freedmen, urban poor, and veterans of the Roman legions.[8] Roman citizens also came to Corinth. They were part of the dominant group that controlled the political and religious institutions of the city while other Romans and Italians belonged to the working class.[9] Though some of the freedmen were likely Greek most of them were Jews, Syrians, Egyptians, Gauls, and from Asia Minor. In particular Roman Corinth had a strong Jewish community.[10] When Caesar went to battle against Pompey the Jews backed him up because he granted them immunity from taxation.[11] It is likely some of them were sent as colonists to Corinth as their reward for their loyalty to Caesar. Philo also attested to the existence of a large Jewish community in Corinth.[12] It is thought that they were composed of "few Roman citizens, ship owners, ship workers, artisans, merchants and slaves."[13] There were Greeks who migrated too. Some of them had obtained Roman citizenship while others had not.[14] Those who were granted Roman citizenship became the elite or the provincial ruling class because they were appointed as administrative officers such as members of the

---

4. Murphy-O'Connor, *St. Paul's Corinth*, 43; Engels, *Roman Corinth*, 16.
5. Bookidis, "Religion in Corinth," 150–51.
6. de Vos, *Church and Community Conflicts*, 182.
7. Walters, "Civic Identity," 402–3.
8. Strabo, *Geogr.* 8.6.23.
9. Engels, *Roman Corinth*, 67–69.
10. Vos, *Church and Community Conflicts*, 187.
11. Stambaugh and Balch, *New Testament*, 16.
12. Philo, *De Leg.* 281–82.
13. Witherington, *Conflict and Community*, 27.
14. Walters, "Civic Identity," 403.

senate.[15] The non-Roman citizens of the city, many of whom were probably Greeks from neighboring towns and provinces, were classified as *incolae*. As non-citizens of the colony "they could not vote, hold magistracies, or be members of the curia unless they were given a special grant of citizenship."[16] Other non-Roman citizens who came to Corinth were Anatolians and Phoenicians.[17]

Bookidis suggests that when Corinth was reestablished there were no original Corinthians in the city anymore. She argues it is unlikely that the original residents of Corinth came back after the destruction because there are no evidences from excavations that show they continued the cultic practices. Thus, those who occupied Corinth at the time of its rebuilding were not original inhabitants but probably squatters who were serving the "interests of Roman exploiters of the land."[18] However, some scholars argue that among those who reoccupied Corinth were believed to be descendants of the Greek remnants. Those who survived the war and who fled the city before Mummius destroyed it were believed to have returned to the city after the destruction. Richard Oster Jr. affirms it is highly probable the remnants resumed their commercial, cultural, and religious practices even before its refounding in 44 BC.[19] Cicero, who visited Corinth between 79–77 BC, attests that Corinth was not completely deserted by its residents. He describes how the Corinthian residents managed to survive the traumatic effects of the destruction of the city. He writes,

> But by the time I saw them they had ceased, it may be, to chant dirges. Their features, speech, their movements, and postures would have led one to say they were freemen of Argos or Sicyon; and at Corinth the sudden sight of the ruins of Corinth had more effect on me than the actual inhabitants; for long contemplation had had hardening effect upon their souls.[20]

---

15. Woolf, "Becoming Roman," 116–43. Engels notes that among those Greeks who were granted citizenship by Roman magistrates was Julius Cesar. See Engels, *Roman Corinth*, 68.

16. Engels, *Roman Corinth*, 70.

17. Engels, *Roman Corinth*, 70.

18. Bookidis, "Religion in Corinth," 150.

19. Oster, "Use, Misuse and Neglect," 52–73; Engels, *Roman Corinth*, 16, 94. Corinth probably "served as the principal market, and probably continued to serve as an exchange-center though on a greatly reduced scale." See Murphy-O'Connor, *St. Paul's Corinth*, 43–46.

20. Cicero, *Tusc. Disp.* 3.53.

Engels adds that one of the persuasive proofs of the presence of the descendants of the original residents is that Corinth became renowned again for its alloy creations particularly the "Corinthian Bronze" after it was rebuilt. Prior to its destruction in 146 BC, Corinth was a producer of a high-tin bronze alloy. Since this high-tin bronze alloy was unique to Corinth only the Corinthian bronze-workers knew how to manufacture it. After the destruction of Corinth some of these Corinthian bronze-workers were probably sold to slavery and brought to Italy along with the booty. It was there that the Corinthian Bronze was manufactured, an alloy of gold, silver, and bronze. Tradition tells that Corinthian Bronze originated from an accidental melting of the statues of bronze, gold, and silver that Mummius plundered from Corinth. Probably, the descendants of the Corinthian Bronze workers who continued the trade were brought back to Corinth when it was rebuilt and continued the manufacturing of bronze products.[21]

In the course of time, it was observed that the city's ethnic composition began to shift from Latin to Greek. In the early days of the Roman colonization many inscriptions, tombstones, and texts bore more Latin names than Greek names prior to the reign of Hadrian. Over the years, many extant inscriptions, tombstones, and texts indicated the declining Latin influence and the increasing Greek dominance.[22] During Favorinus's visit to Corinth in the second century he commented that Corinth had become "thoroughly Hellenized."[23] Engels writes,

> Further evidence for a change in ethnic composition comes from the names of the makers of Corinthian terra sigillata ware. From the founding of the city to the mid-first century A.D., the potters had Latin names written in the Latin alphabet; after that date, Greek names in the Greek alphabet are found, indicating a change in the makers and market. Since these locally produced imitations were not exported in quantity, the change in names indicates a change in the ethnic composition of Corinth. During the first century A.D., the column bases, moldings, and architectural ornaments of Corinth's buildings change from the

---

21. Engels, *Roman Corinth*, 16, 36–37, 70.
22. Engels, *Roman Corinth*, 71; Vos, *Church and Community Conflicts*, 183.
23. Dio Chrysostom, [*Cor.*] 37.26.

Roman to the Greek tradition, which indicates at least a change in the public taste, if not a change in the ethnic origin of the marble-workers themselves. Finally, the religious preferences among Corinth's population changed during the first three centuries A.D. In this era, the inscriptions reveal a decline in the importance of specifically Roman cults and an increase in native Greek religions.[24]

How did this happen? First, the primary factor was the growing influence of the Greek culture. Greek-speaking merchants and tourists patronized the city of Corinth. There was a gradual increase of Greek migrants too from neighboring regions who were recruited to work in different city services. Second, mortality rates were higher than the birth rates in the overcrowded urban settlements. As a bustling city frequented by guests of all kinds from all over the Mediterranean region Corinth was undoubtedly exposed to a lot of communicable diseases including tuberculosis, measles, typhoid, cholera, malaria, venereal disease, and others. Most likely this phenomenon had affected primarily the urban residents which were predominantly Italian during that time. Though Corinth had public health services the extent of the number of residents and visitors affected were beyond what they could manage. Third, another problem that Corinth faced was the lack of food supply. Local food production could not sustain the huge crowd swarming the city regularly. The limited capability of both sea and land transportation made it difficult to import enough food for everyone in the city. Rural residents had greater chances of survival because they grew their own food products. This situation greatly affected the urban citizen's health resistance capability against infectious diseases. They became vulnerable to these diseases and many of them died not of famine but of illnesses.[25]

It must be noted, however, that when Corinth was rebuilt "it was thoroughly Roman in its character and ethos."[26] It was given an almost total facelift not

---

24. Engels, *Roman Corinth*, 72.

25. Engels, *Roman Corinth*, 71–76. Bruce Winter attests that Corinth experienced famine at least three times. During those days, even the rumor of famine had already caused social unrest and price hike. To solve the problem, the city officials appointed a superintendent of the grain supply, *curator annonae*, to supply the market with cheap grain so people would have food and price would have gone down. See Winter, *After Paul Left*, 6.

26. Vos, *Church and Community Conflicts*, 182.

only in terms of its structural and architectural design but also in terms of its political structure and social and religious life.[27] Winter affirms that Corinth was modernized to display Roman identity, not a restoration of the classical Greek city. Temples were altered to imitate Roman temple conventions. The colonists made sure that the new Roman Corinth bore no resemblance to the old Greek city indicating the discontinuity of the former Greek city and the rise of the new Roman colony. In fact, they gave the city a Latin name to emphasize her new identity. Some of the Greek notables were Romanized. They were awarded Roman citizenship and given provincial administrative offices. Thus, at the early part of the colonization Roman culture was more dominant than Greek culture and any other cultures.[28]

Greg Woolf explains that despite living within the Roman culture the Greeks managed to keep their cultural identity, that is, they "remained Greeks while using Roman things."[29] It is possible the Greek community was exposed to Roman religious and cultural practices – like the impact of the institution of imperial cults where they celebrated imperial festivals annually, which were partly highlighted by the holding of *venationes* and the related gladiatorial combats.[30] However, Greeks were careful to select only those ones that were compatible to their culture. They kept their language, religion, and cultural norms while engaging with the social and cultural life of the Roman city. It was neither a case of defiance nor accommodation of the Roman culture. Rather, they were able to keep their heritage because the Romans tolerated it. The Romans allowed them to maintain Greek customs. Thus, Hellenism survived. Woolf explains, "Romans let Greeks alone or even favoured them to the extent of ceding the east to Hellenism, while they Romanized the west."[31] Walters also contends that the Romanization of the notables helped the spread of Greek culture. As the local decurions, they were given the responsibility to administer the affairs of the colony including its religious practices, that is, "to select, organize, and arrange the finances of civic cults."[32] This development

---

27. Vos, *Church and Community Conflicts*, 182.
28. Winter, *After Paul Left*, 8–22.
29. Woolf, "Becoming Roman," 126–28.
30. Spawforth, "Achaean Federal Court," 151–68, this article is an extract of the longer work of Spawforth, "Corinth, Argos and the Imperial Cult," 211–32.
31. Woolf, "Becoming Roman," 127–31.
32. Walters, "Civic Identity," 409.

affected not only the rise of the Greek culture but also more importantly the socioreligious life of Corinth too.

Strabo noted that Caesar saw Corinth's potential due to its "favorable" geographical location.[33] Indeed, Corinth hosted a multitude of visitors who swarmed the city to behold its beauty and enjoy its irresistible major attractions.[34] As such, Corinth became the hub of attraction in the region because of its entertainment, educational opportunities, religious festivities, commerce, and trading services.

At Corinth, grammar schools, primary schools, and schools of rhetoric proliferated in the city where many of the children of wealthy families studied. Both resident and transient philosophers as well as rhetoricians were frequent guests who gave life to the intellectual and social life of the city.[35] To promote philosophy and rhetoric, especially among the youth, they erected a monument for Favorinus.[36]

---

33. Strabo, *Geogr.* 8.6.23. Cf. Murphy-O'Connor, *St. Paul's Corinth*, 66; Engels, *Roman Corinth*, 17. Another probable reason could also be that Cesar considered Corinth as key to his successful campaign in the region due to its strategic location in the Isthmus.

34. Aristeides testified to the prominence of Corinth in the Mediterranean region. Speaking about the tourist traffic as well as the dynamics of life at Corinth, Aristeides wrote (as quoted and translated by Engels),

> Everything travels here from every place by land and sea, and it is because of this that the ancient poets sang of this place as wealthy, and also because of the delights always present and the happiness that always resides in it. For it is like the marketplace, the common meeting place and festival of the Greeks, which they crowd into, not every two years, as for the present festival, but every year and every day. And if, just as among men, there was the institution of guest-friendship among cities, then this city [Corinth] would be honored everywhere, for it hospitably receives everyone and bids them farewell again. It is the common refuge of all, just as some passageway and crossroads of all mankind, the common city of the Greeks . . . their metropolis . . . What better proof could one make for the magnitude [of the city] than that it has been apportioned into all seas and colonized and settled from them, not from one or another, but from all of them alike. And the city is well governed, an administrative center, and still arbitrates justice among the Greeks. Indeed, such an abundance of wealth and prosperity pours into the city from every land and every sea, that they dwell in the midst of plenty that washes around them, just as some merchant ship filled with valuable cargo . . . Which Greek city is still commemorated as the most brilliant in peace and war, esteemed by land and sea? Which is the most conspicuous in deeds and accomplishments? But the present era is peaceful . . . and when the Greeks celebrate festivals, they live in harmony together in this most splendid and renowned celebration [the Isthmian Games].

See Engels, *Roman Corinth*, 79.

35. Engels, *Roman Corinth*, 43–49.

36. Dio Chrysostum, [*Cor.*]. 37.8. The Sophistic activities of the first century shall be discussed more extensively below.

Corinth's entertainment industry also provided popular attractions in the city. Theatrical and musical performances abounded in the city. Corinth boasted of magnificent odeon and amphitheaters that could hold tens of thousands of spectators where gladiatorial contests and games were held. Corinth celebrated three major games: the biennial Isthmian, the quadrennial Caesarian, and the Imperial. The Isthmian games consisted of literary and musical contests, hippic contests (horse races and chariot maneuverings), and athletic events (pentathlon, racing, boxing and wrestling). The Caesarian games and Imperial contests consisted of encomia for the imperial family, poetry, and singing contests.[37]

Religion played significant role in the life of the city. Among the top considerations of the Roman Corinth at that time was to provide sufficient religious services for the residents as well as guests to the city. People from different places had access to various religious festivals and practices because the religious atmosphere of Corinth catered to people of various ethnic and cultural as well as religious backgrounds, whether Greeks, Jews, Egyptians, or Romans. These religious festivities also included the processions like the processions of the cult of Isis and Serapis. Temples were rededicated and shrines were built to allow worshippers of different cults to perform rites like initiation rites for the cult of Demeter and Kore as well as the worship rites for the cult of Asklepios.[38] Among the popular gods revived was Poseidon/Neptune, the god of the sea and earthquake, in whose honor the Isthmian games were regularly celebrated. Also, many inscriptions and dedications were attributed to Aphrodite/Venus.[39] Other gods and cults include Apollo, Athena, Ephesian Artemis, Hermes/Mercury, Jupiter Capitolinus, Tyche/Fortuna, Zeus, the Egyptian cults (Isis and Serapis), Imperial cult and the Genius of the Colony.[40] Several bathing and exercise facilities were located

---

37. Engels, *Roman Corinth*, 47–52.

38. Engels, *Roman Corinth*, 43–44. Some of the essential projects undertaken at that time were the rebuilding of three Greek temples which were rededicated to the same divinities in the Roman period: Demeter and Kore, Asklepios and Hygeia, and Aphrodite on Acrocorinth. See Engels, *Roman Corinth*, 94.

39. It is said that the goddess Aphrodite/Venus was considered popular because of the immorality in Corinth and her sacred prostitutes but there is no evidence to prove that this phenomenon was continued when Corinth was re-founded. Though Roman Corinth offered the services of prostitutes, it was not the only immoral city in the region at that time. See Vos, *Church and Community Conflicts*, 192; Engels, *Roman Corinth*, 97.

40. Vos, *Church and Community Conflicts*, 192–93.

near its temples because some Greek cult worship practices required bathing and exercises at the shrines.[41]

The varied nature of the religious atmosphere at Corinth was not only due to its mixed ethnic composition but also to its political situation at that time. Since the political and religious lives of the people were interrelated the political set up affected the religious climate too. When Corinth was colonized the political governance was centralized under the Imperial administration. Under this system some Greek notables were appointed to political offices to serve as *decurions* and magistrates. As local officials their responsibilities included the administration of the religious life of the city. This set up led to the rise of various religious opportunities. It gave people more freedom to choose their own religious identity as it pleased them because political control of the religious life of the people had slowly declined.[42] Winter explains that the institution of the imperial cult was not strictly imposed on everyone especially on other religious associations in the city like the Corinthian church.[43] Engels observes that the "religious unity of the independent city-state was no longer as important, now that it was only a small part of a vast empire."[44] Walter's summary explains the impact of this religious development on the socioreligious life of Corinth.

> When Corinth was refounded as a Roman colony, the Greek civic identity of old Corinth was destroyed. The civic identity of the new city was initially strongly Roman, reflecting the blueprint of its colonial charter and its predominate Roman population. But the civic identity of Roman Corinth was changing rapidly during the first century C.E., and these changes resulted in a growing ambiguity in the population's civic religious identity, producing decurions and magistrates who were less likely to police private religious associations in the city. This resulted in a socioreligious context in which private religious associations and their members were not viewed with the same level of suspicion

---

41. Engels, *Roman Corinth*, 47.
42. Walters, "Civic Identity," 410.
43. Winter, "Achaean Federal Imperial Cult," 169–78.
44. Engels, *Roman Corinth*, 92–93.

with which they would have been viewed in other cities – like Thessalonike, for example.⁴⁵

As noted above, Corinth became a haven to large numbers of visitors including merchants and sailors owing to its strategic location on the Isthmus. It was a preferred route for merchants and travelers from Italy and Asia because navigating through the treacherous seas in Sicily, the high seas, and the sea beyond Malea proved to be very difficult and dangerous.⁴⁶ In addition it was also a convenient port of call because of its large (and small) harbors along with its great lighthouse and roadway system called *Diolkos*.⁴⁷ Most merchants had their cargos unloaded at Corinth, transported across the Isthmus via the long stretch of *Diolkos* and reloaded at the other end of the Isthmus to avoid sailing through the dangerous seas of Cape Malea. Despite its high cost due to the large manual labor required to haul these cargos most merchants still preferred this transport system because it was safer. It was also more practical because it saved them a six-day boat trip. While having their stopover in the city they took advantage of the services found in the city like food, lodging, numerous entertainments, and religious services (worship to the marine gods, Poseidon and Isis). Doubtless, guests who preferred to live outdoors while attending the Isthmian games bought or rented tents which boosted Corinth's tent making industry too. Some of the wealthy visitors availed themselves of the services of slaves and prostitutes.⁴⁸ As these frequent guests traded with the local market various goods were

---

45. Walters, "Civic Identity," 409–10.

46. Strabo, *Geogr.* 8.6.20. Cf. Engels, *Roman Corinth*, 50.

47. *Diolkos* was a paved six-kilometer roadway connecting both ends of the Isthmus that used trolleys to transport heavy cargoes including smaller vessels and warships. It was built by Periander sometime in the sixth century BC. See Sanders, "Urban Corinth," 13–14.

48. Engels, *Roman Corinth*, 50–59; Describing the sensual life at Corinth, Aristedeis wrote (as quoted and translated by Engels),

> And furthermore, there is no place where one might stay and rest as in the Mother of Seas [Corinth], no place is sweeter or friendlier, or offers such repose, refuge, and a place of safety for all that come to her. But clearly, her beauties, her passions, and her erotic pleasures attract many, as all are bound by pleasure, and all alike are kindled by her to find love, passion, companionship, and allurements. She beguiles their spirit and the wits from them . . . with the enchantments of the goddess, for clearly this is Aphrodite's city.

Engels, *Roman Corinth*, 89.

imported to Corinth and some local products were also exported to other places. So, Corinth became the center of commerce and trade.[49]

Just as Caesar saw the economic prospects of Corinth when he founded it, Paul may have seen its ministry potential too.[50] Most likely Paul may have intentionally joined the crowd of people who came to witness the events in Corinth and interacted with them as part of his strategy of establishing the kingdom work in this budding city.[51]

When Paul ministered in Corinth the Jewish couple Aquila and Priscilla who were tentmakers like him assisted him. Paul's allusion to the presence of Jews in the Corinthian church is primarily because, when Paul ministered in Corinth, he spent a lot of time interacting to these people (Acts 18:4). Despite the hostile treatment he received from the Jewish community Paul had a fruitful ministry where many people believed in the Lord and were baptized including Titius Justus, a worshipper of God, and the synagogue leader Crispus and his household (Acts 18:8). Aside from 1 Corinthians 1:22–24 other Jewish references are found in 1 Corinthians 7:18 (circumcision) and 9:8–10 (Torah). According to de Vos, the names mentioned in 1 Corinthians could be an indicator (though not conclusive) that the church may have been composed of Jews, Greeks, and Romans such as the Latin names Crispus, Fortunatus, and Gaius. Some Greek names are also mentioned like Stephanas and Chloe.[52] In 1 Corinthians 1:23 Paul mentions the Gentiles, which refers to the other minority ethnic groups in the church. Winter argues that the term Ἕλληνες in 1 Corinthians 1:22 can be taken as synonymous of the term ἔθνεσιν in 1 Corinthians 1:23. He claims this is a common synonym for the word Gentiles.[53] However, Paul's use of the words Ἕλληνες in 1 Corinthians 1:22 and ἔθνεσιν in 1 Corinthians 1:23 appears to be intentional especially since in 1 Corinthians 1:24 he uses the term Greeks again. There appears to be no significant point in interposing the term ἔθνεσιν between Ἕλληνες and

---

49. Sanders, "Urban Corinth," 15.
50. Engels, *Roman Corinth*, 20.
51. Stambaugh and Balch, *New Testament*, 158; Broneer, "Apostle Paul," 2–31.
52. Vos, *Church and Community Conflicts*, 196–97. Timothy Brookins notes though there is no indication in the text that suggests she is not part of the Corinthian church. Since she did not need any introduction, it is assumed the Corinthian believers knew her. See Brookins, "Wise Corinthians," 104–52.
53. For full discussion of his view see Winter, *After Paul Left*, 23–25.

Ἕλλησιν if Paul meant it to be understood synonymous only. It makes a lot of sense if we take Ἕλληνες in 1 Corinthians 1:22 as Greeks and ἔθνεσιν in 1:23 as Gentiles especially in view of the church social structure and patronage practices that will be explained below. Here Paul uses the term Ἕλληνες in 1 Corinthians 1:22 and 1:24 in relation to σοφία.

2.2 The Social Structure in Roman Corinth

The political structure of the Roman government sketches the social structure of Corinth where power and status were reserved for the elite. Generally, in the Roman Empire society was divided in two major classes, the upper class and lower class. Corinth, as a Roman colony, was under the rule of the Roman emperor who sits at the top of the upper-class hierarchy. Under the emperor were members of the imperial household, key officials in the central administration, the ordo senatorius (senatorial order), the ordo equester (equestrian order, the wealthy Roman citizen landowners), governors, proconsuls, the ordines decurionum (the orders of decurions, the ruling elite or local aristocrats in the provinces and cities who were merchants, landowners, and manufacturers). These people controlled the political and economic life of the empire. The lower class was composed of the small landowners, craftsmen, shopkeepers, Roman centurions as well as soldiers, merchants, and traders like tentmakers. At the lower strata of the lower class were Roman citizens who had no property and had to work in farms or in construction in order to survive. Some of them depended on their patrons to survive while others chose to steal or beg. At the bottom of the lower class were the slaves who were considered as property according to Roman law.[54]

The senators occupied high offices in the administration of the empire and military.[55] By the end of the first century senators were involved in sociocultural projects and tasked to fulfill ceremonial priesthood.[56] The equestrians were also given posts in the military command. Unlike the senators their numbers were not limited. Criteria for membership include not only birth and legal status but also wealth. In this case the emperor could appoint

---

54. Stambaugh and Balch, *New Testament*, 110–13.
55. Horrell, *Social Ethos*, 65.
56. Stambaugh and Balch, *New Testament*, 111.

a citizen of free birth as an equestrian, provided he had acquired great wealth. The equestrians were tasked to oversee the financial administration and the distribution of food in Rome and the imperial fleets. They also administered small provinces that did not require huge military operations such as the province of Judea in AD 6 to 41 and AD 44 to 66.[57] The decurions were tasked to govern the civic communities, which included collecting taxes, administering harbors and markets, and undertaking embassies to governors and kings.[58]

Membership to the elite strata was primarily based on birth and legal status (Roman citizenship).[59] As a general rule, unless people had inherited their high social status on the basis of birth and legal status, people with "humble origins" knew that their roots were "generally a barrier to progress and a social stigma, even for an individual who managed to amass considerable wealth."[60]

This was the case for some freedmen who were classified under the lower class despite being wealthy. Despite being manumitted, freedmen were continually under the dominion and authority of their owner. In a sense the freedmen enjoyed only limited freedom and remained obligated to their owners. According to the law they were legally bound to continue to render services, submission, and respect. At the same time the owner was legally bound to provide and care for them as needed.[61] Many new citizens who were freedmen in Corinth became rich because they got involved in Italian industry and commerce.[62] David Horrell notes that though these freedmen were wealthy they were not naturally qualified to hold offices.[63]

---

57. Gager, *Kingdom and Community*, 99–100.

58. Stambaugh and Balch, *New Testament*, 111.

59. Gager, *Kingdom and Community*, 97. Though wealth and place of origin were also important these are not the basic criteria for admission to the ruling class.

60. Horrell, *Social Ethos*, 65.

61. Horrell, *Social Ethos*, 66. In reference to the freedmen, Strabo calls them a "freedman class." See Strabo, *Geogr.* 8.6.23; Wallace-Hadrill, "Patronage in Roman Society," 76–77. John K. Chow likened this relationship to a father and son relationship where the father continues to exercise authority over his son. As a client, the freedman must continue to serve his patron. He was expected to continually show loyalty and gratitude to his patron for the freedom he owed from him. Under the law, a freedman cannot sue his patron in court. As patron, the owner was expected to continually extend help like giving him food if the freedman was in need. He was expected to provide his family legal assistance like when his client was murdered or gets involved in cases. At any rate, though his freedom was limited, manumission was the only way a slave could get a better life. For more discussion on this aspect, see Chow, *Patronage and Power*, 70–72.

62. Engels, *Roman Corinth*, 67.

63. Horrell, *Social Ethos*, 66.

Slaves were also part of the lower class, but had a variety of conditions. Many slaves in the rural areas had to survive life in a harsher environment, such as longer hours of work, uncomfortable living conditions, and poverty. On the other hand, slaves in the city had more privileges and opportunities than those in the rural areas. Slaves who helped produce profit in trade and commerce had more freedom than others. Urban slaves had opportunities to possess wealth and obtain higher status than other slaves if they occupied key responsibilities in their master's household, especially those who were working in the imperial household.[64]

Given the ethnic and economic profile of Roman Corinth it is reasonable to postulate that the church was also composed of people of different social status. In 1 Corinthians 1:26–28, Paul alludes that the Corinthian church is composed of people of different social levels, the minority group of the more privileged well-to-do individuals (wise, influential, and noble birth) and the majority group of the lower class of the society.

At the outset Judge issues a caution against uncritically classifying the Christian community according to Roman social classes. While this may be probable it has to be verified by understanding not only society at that time and the Christians' identity but also their function, purpose, and influence in the society. That is, we need to "examine their activities and objectives and the place they occupied in the community."[65]

The early popular view as endorsed by Adolf Deissmann is that the first believers belonged to the most underprivileged group of the Roman society, that is, the first Christian community represented a movement of lower classes.[66] Justin Meggitt also places them in the lowest level whose lives had been constantly rocked by the lack of material security like the urban poor, slaves, and laborers. However, Meggitt also affirms that some of the members whom Paul calls the wise, powerful, and noble are more privileged than the others.[67]

Judge notes it is accurate to assume that the first Christians did not have members who belonged to the upper class of Roman society (the Roman aristocrats) because this class was exclusive and in no way would associate

---

64. Garnsey and Saller, *Roman Empire*, 119. Cf. 124.
65. Judge, "Early Christians," 4–15.
66. Meeks, *First Urban Christians*, 52.
67. Meggitt, *Paul, Poverty, and Survival*, 97–106.

themselves with any local cult. While they may have interacted with some individuals of high social status in social functions it is most likely such interactions happened only among Romanized local officials.[68]

On the other hand, Paul's statement in 1 Corinthians 1:26 clearly indicates a mix of status. Many of them are poor as implied by the fact that they are not wise, powerful, or noble. But the same statement also implies that some are more privileged than the others. This is what John Gager calls the "disprivileged" group. He argues that social deprivation was not based solely on economic condition but on ethnic background, place of origin, gender (women received less privileges and recognition than men), and intellectual or educational achievement. The first Christians may have belonged to the "disprivileged" group but it does not put them at the level of the slaves and the poorest in the society.[69] In his book *The Ancient Economy*, Moses Finley demonstrates the complexity of determining social level in the ancient world. Socioeconomic factors cannot be depended on alone as the primary basis of structuring the ancient society into different classes because it is inseparably linked to political, family origins, religious, and other social factors. Finley writes,

> There is little agreement among historians and sociologists about the definition of "class" or the canons by which to assign anyone to a class. Not even the apparently clearcut, unequivocal Marxist concept of class turns out to be without difficulties. Men are classed according to their relation to the means of production, first between those who do and those who do not own the means of production; second, among the former, between those who work themselves and those who live off the labour of others. Whatever the applicability of that classification in present-day society, for the ancient historian there is an obvious difficulty: the slave and the free wage labourer would then be members of the same class, on a mechanical interpretation, as would the richest senator and the non-working owner of a

---

68. Judge, *Social Pattern*, 52–53.
69. Gager, *Kingdom and Community*, 94–96; Wuellner, "Sociological Implications," 672.

small pottery. That does not seem a very sensible way to analyse ancient society.⁷⁰

Meeks affirms Finley's view. In his article "The Social Context of Pauline Theology" he adopts the concept of "status inconsistency."⁷¹ Based on this he argues for an extensive and multifaceted method of structuring the social level of the first Christians. Our degree of understanding people's social level depends on the measure we use. That is, one's social level cannot just be measured according to their economic status only because ancient society had various ways of ranking one's social status like family origins, occupation, citizenship, educational attainment, and gender (male or female). One could be rich and educated but if they do not come from a prestigious family their social status and rank might still be low. So, determining the social status or rank must be done in different ways. To achieve this, some considerations must be observed. First, education, profession, and economic capability have different values in social ranking. Second, personal perception of one's social rank could be different from others.⁷²

Judge suggests that the Corinthian church was a mixed minority group of affluent city household owners and patrons and the majority group of "household dependents" of these leading members of the church (1 Cor 1:26; 4:8–10; 7:20–24). In a society where the slaves and peasants are considered the lowest class Judge writes, "The dependent members of city household were by no means the most debased section of society. If lacking freedom, they still enjoyed security and a moderate prosperity. The peasantry and persons in slavery on the land were the most underprivileged classes. Christianity left them largely untouched."⁷³ In a sense the Corinthian church was not a

---

70. Finley, *Ancient Economy*, 49.
71. Meeks, "Social Context," 268.
72. Meeks, "Social Context," 268–69; Meeks, *First Urban Christians*, 54–55.
73. Judge, *Social Pattern*, 60; Judge, "Social Identity," 118–21. Judge came up with a short survey of recent scholarship on this issue. According to his survey, initially some scholars like J. J. Nicholls and Paul G. Yule criticized Judge. But it did not draw a lot of reactions because few years later H. Kreissig and M. Hengel came up with similar findings about the mixed composition of the early Christian community. In 1974, Theissen conducted his own study and concluded that both views may have existed during that time as society then was composed of many levels or structures. A similar work on the same year by B. Grimm revealed that tensions or social discriminations between these social structures might have existed at that time.

movement of lower-class people but a "movement sponsored by local patrons to their social dependents."[74]

Paul faced opposition as he was preaching the gospel. In Acts 13:50, after the word of God spread and many people believed in God, the Jewish leaders incited the God-fearing women of high standing as well as the leading men in the city and as result Paul and Barnabas were sent away. In Acts 14:19 some Jews persuaded the crowd against Paul so they stoned Paul and dragged him outside of the city thinking that he was already dead. But the disciples took care of him until he recovered. Notwithstanding the troubles he experienced in those days, opposition did not hinder Paul because he had the support of some converts. In Acts 16:13–15, Paul was teaching a group of women and Lydia, a dealer of purple cloth, was moved by the message of Paul. After she was baptized, together with her household, she invited Paul to stay in her house. In Acts 17:1–9, Paul again reasoned with the people in the synagogue and many people believed including some Jews, God-fearing Greeks, and some prominent women. Jason, one of those who were moved by the message and likely a wealthy person, hosted Paul and his companions in his home.

In relation to Paul's ministry in Corinth, biblical references indicate that some members of the Corinthian church belonged to the wealthy group too. Gaius had a house large enough to accommodate the whole congregation of believers (Rom 16:23). He was one of the people baptized by Paul. As a synagogue ruler (Acts 18:8) he was the leader of the Jewish worship particularly the reading of the Scripture and homilies. He was also responsible for the preservation of the synagogue building. As practiced the position of a synagogue ruler was given to those who were financially stable because they were expected to help fund the maintenance works of the synagogues in addition to the contribution of the Jewish community.[75]

Thus, the social status of Paul's converts – which include wealthy patrons, Jews, God-fearing Greeks, synagogue ruler, a member of Aeropagus, and their respective households – show that the community of believers Paul is ministering to, including the ones in Corinth, is a community of people from different social backgrounds. Judge observes that the identities of Paul's converts also attest to the fact that they are not all an underprivileged group

---

74. Judge, "Early Christians," 8.
75. Theissen, *Social Setting*, 73–74.

but "a school of disciples under the instruction of a rabbi, or a devout sect committed to the study and preservation of the law, or finally of a society formed to attend upon the teaching of a travelling preacher."[76] Also, the fact that Paul is able to engage with people in the synagogues about the scriptures indicate that Paul does not only relate to the wealthy and their households but also to the religious people in the synagogues, as well as to the Epicurean and Stoic philosophers.

On the other hand, Paul's teaching on slaves also alludes to the presence of some slaves and freedmen in the church (1 Cor 7:20–24). It is assumed that these slaves were members of the household of some of the wealthy members of the church. Paul's instruction on the weekly collection implies also the socioeconomic status of the church members which fits the range of income from traders to the "small people, not destitute, but not commanding capital either" whose income or salary was received weekly (1 Cor 16:1–4).[77] Because of the urban setting of Paul's ministry no reference also can be found about members who belong to the lowest class or the most destitute like the poorest of the poor, peasants, agricultural slaves, and hired agricultural day laborers. Meeks explains,

> There may well have been members of the Pauline communities who lived at the subsistence level, but we hear nothing of them. The levels in between, however, are well represented. There are slaves, although we cannot tell how many. The "typical" Christian . . . is a free artisan of small trader. Some even in those occupational categories had houses, slaves, the ability to travel, and other signs of wealth. Some of the wealthy provided housing, meeting places, and other services for individual Christians and for whole groups. In effect, they filled the roles of patrons.[78]

---

76. Judge, "Early Christians: Part II," 136.
77. Meeks, *First Urban Christians*, 57–66.
78. Meeks, 73.

2.3 Patronage in Roman Corinth

The social structure of Corinth reflects a culture of domination by the elite. They were given more privileges in social gatherings like front seats in shows and bigger allocations of food and wine during times the government distributed aid to the constituents.[79] In the legal system of Corinth the elite also enjoyed better access to the legal services in courts due to their social and financial status.[80] They had legal protection from being sued by those who belong to the lower classes. When found guilty of crime the elite were meted lighter punishments.[81] Slaves were penalized with harsher punishments.[82] In fact crucifixion was reserved for slaves, the worst criminals, insurrectionists, and prisoners of war. Those who belong to the lower class may be stripped of their freedom and sold as slaves or made gladiators.[83]

The domination of the elite had some good advantages to the society though. Many of the elite especially those elected into positions as administrators of the city were responsible for the uplifting of the welfare of the people. They sponsored building constructions and entertainments (e.g. Isthmian games). They also hosted public banquets and distributed money among the needy constituents. They also made sure that food was available at an affordable price. Their philanthropic benevolence was said to be unparalleled as attested by numerous honorary inscriptions on the remains of the buildings they funded.[84]

As such Corinth's hierarchical social structure allows patronage to thrive seamlessly. As generally practiced patronage is a social structure that provides the patron and client various opportunities to earn favors and services. A patron was usually a person with great financial resources, social and political influence, who provided goods and services to a client who in return ascribed loyalty and social honor out of obligation or gratitude. It is a social relationship that binds the patron and the client according to their own interests and motivations through the exchange of services and resources. In any case they

---

79. Stambaugh and Balch, *New Testament*, 113.
80. Horrell, *Social Ethos*, 69–70.
81. Stambaugh and Balch, *New Testament*, 113.
82. Garnsey and Saller, *Roman Empire*, 118.
83. Stambaugh and Balch, *New Testament*, 35–36.
84. Engels, *Roman Corinth*, 89–90.

engaged in this social interaction because they mutually benefited from it.[85] Richard Saller gives us an overview of patronage. He writes,

> Patronage is founded on the reciprocal relations between patrons and clients. By patron I mean a person who uses his influence to assist and protect some other person, who becomes his "client," and in return provides certain services to his patron. The relationship is asymmetrical, though the nature of the services exchanged may differ considerably. Three vital elements which distinguish a patronage relationship appear in this passage. First, it involves the reciprocal exchange of goods and services. Secondly, to distinguish it from a commercial transaction in the marketplace, the relationship must be a personal one of some duration. Thirdly, it must be asymmetrical, in the sense that the two parties are of unequal status and offer different kinds of goods and services in the exchange – a quality which sets patronage off from friendship between equals.[86]

Patronage works in various ways. Patronage works for political and social advancements as well as livelihood or survival purposes. In ancient Rome the practice of *salutatio* vividly demonstrates the patronage system. Clients acting as *callers* would show up daily at the house of the patron for the morning *salutatio*. Their social significance was indicated according to the order they were received by the patron. On the other hand, the patron's social status is flaunted based on the social standing of their *callers* and the number of *callers* who would show up on their doorstep.[87] These clients or *callers* may also join the patron "on his rounds of public business during the day and applauding his speeches in court."[88] To reciprocate this gesture, the patron would either give them food, some money or an invitation to dinner.[89] A hopeful young

---

85. Vos, "Once a Slave," 89–105.
86. Saller, *Personal Patronage*, 1; Kwon, *1 Corinthians 1–4*, 90–91.
87. Saller, "Patronage and Friendship," 57; Wallace-Hadrill, "Patronage in Roman Society," 65.
88. Garnsey and Saller, *Roman Empire*, 151.
89. Garnsey and Saller, *Roman Empire*, 151.

politician would join the ranks of *callers* during a morning *salutatio* in order to gain favor and appointment to the imperial aristocracy.[90]

The patronage system enabled the emperor to establish his political rule and control over the entire Roman Empire. The emperor appointed whomever he chose to positions and offices. From top to bottom, the emperor chose from among those he knew or who were recommended to him by subordinates he trusted. Everything depended on favors and recommendations. Political dominion was solidified through patronage.[91] At the same time the emperor also used patronage to emphasize his supremacy over the people. He would give handouts to the Roman plebs and to the army. He would supply them with protection, food, money, water, and entertainment. In return the people were expected to give their respect and loyalty.

At the local level the appointed governors also performed the role of a patron. They facilitated the granting of citizenship and honors from Rome. In return, the people in the province would give them gifts, bribes, and other social favors in order to gain business, political, and other material benefits in return.[92] As such the emperor succeeded not only in establishing himself as possessing supreme dominance but also as a "patron sitting at the center of a vast web of resource distribution, granting or denying to individuals and communities status, privilege, favourable hearings and wealth."[93] As suggested by Saller, patronage was one major factor in determining why Roman emperors were able to effectively govern a huge empire without requiring a large administration. Emperors used this structure to sustain dominion over provinces and cities, implement law and order, efficiently collect taxes, provide basic social services for the masses, secure political stability, and other internal administrative functions.[94]

The Roman colony at Corinth benefited from this practice of patronage. Corinth enjoyed protection, peace, prosperity, and the emperor's benefactions. The emperor appointed Roman officials to administer the city. In return Corinth extended to the Roman rulers the title "patron," erected monuments,

---

90. Saller, "Patronage and Friendship," 58.
91. Ste. Croix, *Class Struggle*, 364–65.
92. Garnsey and Saller, *Roman Empire*, 149–52.
93. Wallace-Hadrill, "Patronage in Roman Society," 84.
94. Saller, *Personal Patronage*, 205–6; Hendrix, "Benefactor/Patron Networks," 39–58.

and made inscriptions to honor them. They organized special celebrations and festivals to honor them. Some of the wealthy people gave large donations for the repair of the sanctuary at Isthmia, sponsored the Isthmian games, and other major celebrations.[95] Roman officials took advantage of the friendship and generosity of the wealthy people who befriended the Roman officials to gain greater advantages for their own businesses and political interests. As a result, some of these wealthy people were appointed to administer the city as magistrates or members of the local council.[96] John K. Chow summarizes how patronage worked at Corinth:

> Based on this examination of the lives of some of local notables in Corinth, we gain the following impression of the way relationships were organized in the larger community at Corinth. The populace had to look for the rich to provide them with entertainment like games, to bring a better environment and honour to the city through new buildings, and at times to provide food relief. Honourable offices and honourable titles like "patron" were usually offered to the benefactors in return for their benefactions. There might even be privileges for them to enjoy. Hence, it is almost inevitable that the rich people were often the powerful people in Corinth.[97]

As noted above, Paul was ably assisted by his patrons in his ministries. On several occasions he was hosted in their homes. Lydia invited him and his companions to stay at her house in Acts 16:13–15. In Acts 16:40 after he and Silas got out of prison Lydia welcomed them again to her house where he met with the believers again to encourage them. Jason also hosted him together with his traveling companions in Acts 17:1–9. Priscilla and Aquila also hosted him when he first came to Corinth in Acts 18:4.

These patrons, however, did not only host him but also labored with Paul. In Romans 16:3 Paul talks about how Priscilla and Aquila risked their lives for Paul. In Acts 17:1–9 even Jason, who hosted Paul in Thessalonica, was dragged into trouble and had to post bond so he could be released. It is clear

---

95. Kent, *Corinth*, 70–73; West, *Corinth*, 107–8; Engels, *Roman Corinth*, 68–69.
96. Chow, *Patronage and Power*, 41–62.
97. Chow, 63.

that Paul's patrons participated in the ministry to the point of sacrificing their own safety, if not their own lives, for the sake of the spreading of the gospel.

Though it is not clear that they helped fund the ministry activities of Paul but it is fairly assumed that such practice inevitably existed, probably not by personally giving money to Paul but by attending to his needs and the needs of the house churches, as their private homes were hosts to the church's weekly gatherings. As noted in Acts 20:20 Paul mentions his preaching ministry both in public and in different house churches.[98] As the ministry expanded weekly gatherings could no longer be hosted in one home, and several homes had to be opened to accommodate the growing number of believers. In Romans 16:1–2 Paul mentions Phoebe as the servant and benefactor of the church in Cenchreae. In Corinth believers were hosted in different households of patrons like Justus, Gaius, Crispus, and Stephanas. Aside from occasional times where the entire congregations gathered as a whole church in one place, probably in Gaius's home (1 Cor 14:23; Rom 16:23) most of the time they gathered in several homes of the patrons (1 Cor 11:17–18).[99] In 1 Corinthians 16:15 Paul commends Stephanas and his household for how they labored hard for the service of the Corinthian believers. Priscilla and Aquilla hosted the church in their home according to 1 Corinthians 16:17.

Paul exhorts the Corinthian believers to submit to "such people and to everyone who joins in the work and labors at it" according to 1 Corinthians 16:16. Paul's exhortation to the Corinthians believers denotes some possible implications to how the household churches worked. First, the phrase "such people" in Paul's exhortation to the Corinthian believers in 16:16 refers to Stephanas and his household. Second, Paul's exhortation to the Corinthian believers to submit to Stephanas implies that he holds a position of influence in the church of Corinth. That is, it is likely that Stephanas was a household church patron. James S. Jeffers notes that a household patron was considered a spiritual leader of the household church and members of the congregation were expected to submit to their authority.[100] Third, the phrase "everyone who joins in the work and labors at it" in Paul's exhortation to the Corinthians

---

98. Cf. Stowers, "Social Status," 59–82.

99. Cf. Brookins, *Corinthian Wisdom*, 108–9; Barnett, *Corinthian Question*, 68–69, 89; Lampe, "Paul, Patrons and Clients," 495–97.

100. Jeffers, *Greco-Roman World*, 82–83.

believers in 16:16 is a reference to the other patrons who are also leading other house churches. Since these patrons are mentioned along with Stephanas and his household, it also implies that these patrons are of the same mind and intention with Stephanas. Otherwise, if the phrase "everyone who joins in the work and labors at it" is taken to refer to people who are not patrons, it does not make sense that Paul would urge the Corinthian believers to submit to them too.

It is evident that the household patrons hold a significant influence and authority over the members of the household churches. In this case, it is not difficult to see how the situation in Corinth where house churches that were led by household patrons could have contributed to the problem of division in the Corinthian church.[101] Floyd V. Filson observes that the house church structure during the time of Paul (where many house churches were established in the different parts of the city) is disposed to suffer from quarrels and division. He adds,

> Christians of a certain tendency grouped together and thereby were confirmed in that tendency. Separation from Christians of somewhat different background, views, and interests must have operated to prevent the growth of mutual understanding. Each group had its feelings of pride and prestige. Such a physically divided church tended almost inevitably to become a mentally divided church.[102]

Jeffers also says that the quarreling and division in the church of Corinth are "based in different households."[103]

In view of this, it is possible that the slogans in 1 Corinthians 1:12 "I am of Paul," "I of Apollos," "I of Cephas," and "I of Christ" indicates that the quarreling may have been led by the patrons and supported by the members of the house churches. In addition, Lawrence L. Welborn states that those who are influential and wealthy are the ones leading the quarreling in the church based on the fact that Paul refers to those who examine him as "wise," "strong," and "honored" in 1 Corinthians 4:10.[104]

---

101. Burke, "Paul's Role," 95–114.
102. Filson, "Early House Churches," 105–12.
103. Jeffers, *Greco-Roman World*, 81–82.
104. Welborn, "Discord in Corinth," 85–111.

This situation in the Corinthian church provides preliminary insights into our understanding of how the problems of division, boasting, and wisdom are connected to each other. First, on the problems of division and boasting in the church, the quarreling may have been influenced by the special relationship that existed between the missionary workers and the patrons of the church. Observing the social dynamics in the church, a patron may have developed a special bond with the missionary worker who has visited the house church. It is noted here that it was their practice to host missionary workers in their time. This practice was not only extended to Paul but also to Apollos. In Acts 18:24–28 Apollos arrived in Ephesus after Paul left to visit other disciples in the region of Galatia and Phrygia. When Priscilla and Aquila heard him preach the gospel in Ephesus they invited him to their house and they explained to him the word of God more clearly. Later, when Apollos wanted to proceed to Corinth the believers in Ephesus, who were probably worshipping in the house of Priscilla and Aquila, sent a letter of recommendation to the believers in Corinth so that they might welcome him too. The sending of recommendation letters seems to be a practice among the believers whenever a missionary worker visited another city so that the house church there would also welcome and host him (2 Cor 3:1). It is in this occasion that the special bond between the patrons and missionary workers was probably developed. As one missionary worker was hosted in the home of the household patron as in the case of Paul and Apollos it is almost inevitable that a special relationship developed overtime. In this case, it cannot be avoided that the patron and their household became loyal to the missionary worker. In addition, Paul's reference to baptism in 1 Corinthians 1:13–16 seems to allude to the issue of who baptized their household (who baptized who). Thus, the quarreling was probably related to the patrons' loyalty toward the missionary worker they supported (1 Cor 4:6) who baptized their household. In the case of Paul and Apollos, it is safe to assume that the patrons together with their respective congregations are boasting about Paul and Apollos. In this case, the quarreling existed between house churches that are boasting about their preferred missionary worker.[105]

In addition, Welborn notes also how the social makeup contributed to the problem of division. It is not difficult to connect how the members of

---

105. Theissen, *Social Setting*, 54–57.

the church were dragged into the quarrel. Welborn asserts that since there are many poor people in the church who belong to the lower class it is understandable that they become dependent and loyal on those ones who are "men of substance."[106] Further, Paul refers to those who examine and criticize him as "wise," "strong," and "honored" in 1 Corinthians 4:10. It is probable that these "wise," "strong," and "honored are the influential and wealthy ones who are leading the quarreling in the church.[107] If this observation is granted it is safe to assume that the quarrels are not only between the believers but also primarily between patrons who are leading these house churches whom Paul refers to as the wise, powerful, and noble people in 1 Corinthians 1:26 and 4:10.[108]

Second, on the problem of wisdom, the tension that exists between Paul and some Corinthian believers is probably related to the Corinthians' interest in wisdom and rhetoric. Aside from the influence of the sophistic practices in the first century upon some of the believers (which will be explained below), Apollos influenced some of them when he visited the church few years earlier. In Acts 18:27–19:1, while Paul was in Ephesus, Apollos went to Corinth and ministered among the Corinthian believers. Though it is not clear how long he stayed in Corinth, his ministry among them made an impact in the lives of the believers and also in the community. Apollos was eloquent in speech and knowledgeable with the Scriptures (Acts 18:24–25), that is, he was proficient with the interpretation of Torah. Also, because he was eloquent in speech and knowledgeable with the Scriptures, he was able to refute the Jewish opponents in public debate. As a result, he was instrumental in the growth of the church and the believers were greatly helped in the work at Corinth.

Paul refers to Apollos as his fellow worker so it can be inferred that there was no quarrel between him and Apollos. However, those who were influenced by Apollos are likely criticizing Paul because of his deficiency in rhetorical skills. It is noted as declared by Paul in 1 Corinthians 1:17 that he did not proclaim the gospel using human persuasion. In 1 Corinthians 2:1–5 Paul mentions that he did not come with superiority of speech and wisdom. In fact, he proclaimed the gospel in weakness with fear and trembling. His

---

106. Welborn, "Discord in Corinth," 85–111; Welborn, *Politics and Rhetoric*, 3–32.
107. Welborn, "Discord in Corinth," 85–111.
108. Theissen, *Social Setting*, 54–57; Welborn, "Discord in Corinth," 85–111.

statements allude to the fact that Corinthian believers were criticizing him for his lack of rhetorical skills, and these believers were probably influenced by and exposed to the practice of rhetoric. In 1 Corinthians 4:1–5 it is highly probable that Paul's statement on being examined by the Corinthian believers refer to the criticisms against him about his lack of rhetorical skills. This situation in the Corinthian church has prompted Paul to explain the nature of his preaching ministry and the purpose of his method. Paul wants them to understand that the gospel itself is the power of God that brings salvation to those who believe. In this manner, Paul emphasizes that they received the gospel and believed in the Lord not based on human persuasion but on the power of the Spirit of God.

Thus, as noted above, it is highly probable that the patrons whom Paul calls the wise, powerful or strong, and noble or honorable people mentioned in 1 Corinthians 1:26 and 4:10 and their respective congregations in their household churches are the ones criticizing Paul and boasting about Apollos because they were probably enamored by Apollos's eloquence in rhetoric.

2.4 Sophistic Movement in Roman Corinth during the First Century

The term sophist used to mean wise man but was later expanded during the first century to refer to someone who had acquired and demonstrated excellent skills in rhetoric, the art of persuasion. Because sophists were highly skilled orators and men of high rhetorical caliber they attracted students and earned public respect and following. They would speak about different topics in different social and political functions.[109]

Witherington explains that rhetoric during the early part of the first century was not just a display of linguistic prowess but also a "primary discipline in Roman higher education."[110] It was an essential mode of communication. It was an avenue to "persuade the audience in regard to some future action, to defend some past course of action, or to offer praise or blame about something in the present."[111] Rhetoric became very popular and schools were opened

---

109. Winter, *Philo and Paul*, 3–5.
110. Witherington, *Conflict and Community*, 40.
111. Witherington, *Conflict and Community*, 44.

exclusively for this art. Any student enrolled in this exclusive school was called a disciple (μαθητής), which indicated they were under the mentorship of a sophist.[112] Students were taught regarding different styles, voice control/mechanics, and use of body language. Parents sought this kind of training for their children because they wanted to see them become accomplished rhetoricians in the legal courts, councils, or political assembly of the city. During those days it was seen as a way of preparing and producing the future leaders of the community who would occupy influential positions in the different sectors of the community such as the senators, councilors, officials of the imperial government, and civic as well as provincial ambassadors.[113] It appeared on the basis of its purpose that although the schools of rhetoric were probably not exclusive to the elite it catered primarily to the (children of the) wise, powerful, and noble people mentioned in 1 Corinthians 1:26 who could afford expensive education and have access to the offices coveted above. Unfortunately, sophists abused the art and built a perverted sophistic practice. They indulged into deception and wrangling for personal gain.

Dio Chrysostom had witnessed the proliferation of the sophistic activities at Corinth. He witnessed how the practices of the sophists and their respective disciples had veered away from the intention mentioned above. Though the intentions of the parents above may not be as noble and selfless as it seems (on the contrary it might even be driven by selfish political and personal reasons), the disorder and chaos that Dio Chrysostom observed went beyond the acceptable norm at that time. The sophists were shouting and quarreling against each other. Dio Chrysostom observes, "That was the time, too, when one could hear crowds of wretched sophists around Poseidon's temple shouting and reviling one another, and their disciples, as they were called, fighting with one another, many writers reading aloud their stupid works, many poets reciting their poems while others applauded them."[114]

The sophists served as political spokespersons of high officials in different functions. For a fee they also performed in public places, discussing and declaiming on a wide variety of topics. Because they were highly esteemed and their students were probably mostly from elite families "they ran expensive

---

112. Winter, *After Paul Left*, 33.
113. Winter, *Philo and Paul*, 3–5.
114. Dio Chrysostom, *Or.* 8.9.

schools."¹¹⁵ At that time sophists competed against each other. The competition was so widespread that one could rarely find a sophist who had no enemies, like the prominent sophists Rufus and Perithus. Almost every sophist was locked in dishonorable struggle against others. They hurled disparaging remarks against each other publicly in order to humiliate one another as well as demonstrate their superiority over the opposing sophists.¹¹⁶ The competition between Favorinus and Polemo was seen as a quarrel between two cities, Ephesus and Smyrna, where Ephesus preferred Favorinus and Smyrna admired Polemo.¹¹⁷ Philostratus described the disgraceful act of these sophists. He wrote,

> However they may be forgiven for that rivalry, since human nature holds that the love of glory never grows old; but they are to be blamed for the speeches they composed assailing one another; for personal abuse is brutal, and if even it be true, that does not acquit of disgrace even the man who speaks about such things.¹¹⁸

As such the competition between sophists had gone beyond professional practice to personal attacks as these sophists engaged in public humiliation to vie for prominence and secure their place in the society.

Sophists expected their students to demonstrate great loyalty and zeal toward them. Over time as the perverted practice of sophistic activities continued to cause havoc among the sophists and their disciples the term zealot (ζηλωτής) became synonymous to the term disciple (μαθητής).¹¹⁹ Disciples

---

115. Winter, *After Paul Left*, 32–33.

116. Bowersock, *Greek Sophists*, 89–92. Bowersock has devoted one chapter in this book (chapter 7) to describe the extent of the quarrels between sophists.

117. Favorinus was a student of Chrysostom who became a popular sophist, also spoke of the Corinthian response to the sophistic movement. He spoke of the Corinthians' admiration of the so-called sophists, which was exemplified by no less than his reputation in the city. Indeed, his exceptional eloquence had inspired the Corinthians greatly, both the adults and the youth. Many Corinthians admired him that they erected a Corinthian-bronze of him in order to encourage the youth of Corinth to follow his footsteps. Yet, due to the nature of the sophistic activities at that time, some Corinthians who probably hated him overturned the statue few years later, a disrespectful act he considered as a way of banishing him from the city. See Winter, *Philo and Paul*, 129–36. Cf. Dio Chrysostom, [*Cor.*]. 37.16.

118. Philostratus, *Vit. Soph.* 490–91.

119. Although in some ways, it is used to indicate the degree of relationship a student has with the sophist or teacher and the degree of influence the teacher has over his disciple.

were expected to fully imitate the speech, rhetorical style, and even the bodily movement or language (manner of walking and dressing) of their teachers. This was an essential element of their training in order to demonstrate good stage command. They were expected to promote their teacher's ability, reputation, and defend them against the critics. Unfortunately, like their teachers these students acted in a disgraceful manner not just disrespectfully lambasting other sophists but also hurting fellow students physically in the spirit of misguided loyalty. Winter notes,

> By engaging in verbal battles with other students they were simply following a long-established requirement of demonstrating their exclusive loyalty to their own sophist. Zealousness for one's teacher by promoting his attributes and at the same time openly criticizing the deficiencies of another epitomized the behavior of the disciples of first-century teachers.[120]

The sophistic activities during this time centered on the acquisition of knowledge and skills solely for the purpose of personal gain. Devoid of moral values and birthed in the spirit of pride and competition people sought to be wise in their own reprehensible ways. They stooped so low by engaging in practices that betray the very essence of wisdom.

Just as the squabbles among sophists (and their disciples) created disgraceful competition among the sophists and their followers in society, the quarreling among the Corinthian believers in 1 Corinthians 1–4 was also causing division in the church. Chow notes that though the church was still meeting continually they were probably not living in unity and harmony with each other. How is this possible? As stated above, the church in Corinth is composed of many house churches that are led by wealthy household patrons. So, the regular meeting in each household church is not interrupted even when there is quarreling between house churches.[121]

Apparently when Paul and Apollos ministered in Corinth many people admired their leadership and ministry. In the course of time after Paul and Apollos left Corinth quarrels erupted among them. The Corinthians believers

---

Philostratus described Demosthenes as a disciple (μαθητής) of Isaeus but a zealot (ζηλωτής) of Isocrates. See Philostratus, *Vit. Soph.* 504.

120. Winter, *After Paul Left*, 35–40.
121. Chow, *Patronage and Power*, 94.

were boasting about Paul and Apollos in the same way that the disciples of first-century sophists acted toward one another.

The problems Paul is confronting in the church seem to reflect an almost similar, if not identical, conduct of the disciples of sophists in the society. The behavior of the Corinthian believers who are criticizing Paul while at the same time boasting about their preferred missionary worker seems to reflect the loyalty of first-century disciples. Unlike the sophists, there was no proof that Paul and the other names mentioned in the slogans were part of the quarrels.

There are two specific references when Paul refers to this sophistic-like behavior. First, Paul appeals to the church to agree with one another in 1 Corinthians 1:10. They were saying in 1 Corinthians 1:12 Ἐγὼ μέν εἰμι Παύλου, Ἐγὼ δὲ Ἀπολλῶ, Ἐγὼ δὲ Κηφᾶ, Ἐγὼ δὲ Χριστοῦ. Paul implies that their quarreling is not consistent with the fact that they are one in Christ. Thus, he asks "Has Christ been divided? Paul was not crucified for you, was he? Or were you baptized in the name of Paul?" (1:13). These questions heighten Paul's concern for the unity of the body of Christ. His first response is to appeal to the nature of the body of Christ where, as one body, there is supposed to be no room for quarreling that leads to divisions such as the situation in Corinthian church. He also points out that loyalty to him (or to the other names mentioned in the slogan) that reaches this far where it becomes damaging to the body of Christ is absurd. He was not crucified for anybody so there is no basis for people to even cast their loyalty to him. If there was any reason to boast about somebody or pledge a loyalty to somebody, then it must be Christ for he is the one who was crucified for them. In 1 Corinthians 1:13 it is possible that Paul intentionally mentions his name as a representation of the other names mentioned in 1:12. It is evident in the fact that he referred to himself as "Paul" instead of the possessive pronouns "my" and "his." These statements of Paul are meant to refute the validity of their claims especially in relation to their boastings about their leaders. No leaders were crucified for them and none were baptized in the name of any leader. Just as Christ is not divided, and only Christ was crucified for them as well as the only name they were baptized in, so all of them must unite as one in the name of Jesus Christ our Lord and put all their boastings about their missionary workers aside.

Winter suggests these claims, Ἐγὼ μέν εἰμι Παύλου, Ἐγὼ δὲ Ἀπολλῶ, Ἐγὼ δὲ Κηφᾶ, Ἐγὼ δὲ Χριστοῦ, echo the commitment of the disciple to his teacher.

Here, like any μαθητής of the sophists in Corinth, the Corinthian believers seem to perceive themselves as disciples of the Corinthian worker to whom they have pledged their loyalty.[122] As such, in the same manner that the first-century disciples of sophists demonstrated their loyalty to their respective teachers by fighting with other disciples, the Corinthian believers also expressed their loyalty by boasting about their missionary workers and even quarreling with other believers who support different missionary workers.

Second, in 1 Corinthians 3:3 Paul points out that the quarreling in the church reflects the worldly conduct of people who are not spiritual. Their divisive spirit has become a threat to the unity of the church in the same way that the sophistic activities were splitting the society in favor of their admired sophists. Winter explains that the Corinthian believers have followed the "secular fashion" in evaluating their missionary workers or leaders according to their rhetorical skills.[123]

2.5 Summary

The examination of the Corinthians' social context above presents the following analysis. First, Roman Corinth was a multi-ethnic city largely inhabited by Jews, Greeks, and Romans from its rebuilding in 44 BC. It is difficult though to assess the size of each of these major groups. Considering Paul ministered in Corinth sometime in the middle of the first century, we can assume there was still a reasonable diversity of ethnic representations at that time. It is difficult to establish though how many from each of these groups were members of the Corinthian church. There is limited biblical reference to determine the ratio of ethnic diversity in the church of Corinth. Some Jews who became part of the Corinthian church were Titius Justus, a worshipper of God, and the synagogue leader Crispus and his household (Acts 18:8).

Second, the Corinthian church is composed of members from different social classes. As explicitly mentioned by Paul in 1 Corinthians 1:26 some members belong to the minority group of well-to-do individuals while most members belong to the majority group of the lower class of the society. Gaius had a house large enough to accommodate the whole congregation of

---

122. Winter, *Philo and Paul*, 170–71.
123. Winter, 173.

believers (Rom 16:23). Crispus was highly esteemed in the Jewish community (1 Cor 1:14; Acts 18:8). Stephanas and his household were among the first converts of Paul in Achaia (1 Cor 16:15). Their social background reveals that the church has no members belonging either to the upper class of aristocrats or to the lowest class of the poorest of the poor. It is safe to postulate that the church was composed of traders, artisans, some wealthy patrons and their household dependents.

Third, Paul's ministry was faithfully assisted by some of the wealthy patrons of the church, probably those who were converted in the early days of his ministry in Corinth. Some of these who hosted him also participated faithfully, even risking their lives for the ministry, such as Lydia (Acts 16:13–15, 40), Jason (Acts 17:1–9), Priscilla and Aquila (Acts 18:4), and Stephanas and his household (1 Cor 16:15). They also played key roles as generous hosts to different house churches. They opened their private homes to become a place of gathering for the congregation to meet regularly. We can presume they are the leaders of the house churches based on the fact that Paul mentions their names along with the term "household" whenever he refers to them especially in his commendations in Romans 16 and 1 Corinthians 16. As the generous hosts and leaders of the house churches patrons probably earned the respect and loyalty of those who were meeting in their homes. Thus, they were very influential in their respective house churches and the entire Corinthian church. There is a greater probability their influence over their respective house churches may have contributed to how the quarreling affected other members of the congregation or other house churches. It is often assumed that the problems involved the members of the church only. Considering the structure in the house churches where the patrons were the leaders of the house churches it is more consistent to assert that the problems, particularly the boasting and quarreling, may have started among the patrons. As stated above, patrons had greater chance of nurturing close ties with the missionary workers or leaders. Paul's reference to baptism implies that the missionary worker also baptized the patron's household. So, when the boastings and quarreling erupted among the patrons the members of their respective house churches followed suit. Soon the boasting and criticizing reached the other house churches and they too joined in boasting about their preferred missionary worker and criticizing the other one.

Fourth, the problems in the church demonstrate a conduct similar to the sophistic quarrels in the first century. Sophists along with their loyal disciples were competing and quarreling against each other. In the same manner, the Corinthian believers are boasting about their preferred missionary worker, criticizing the other, and quarreling against each other. They are quarreling because they probably see themselves as loyal disciples of the missionary workers in the same way that the students of rhetoric consider themselves as disciples of the sophists.

Finally, the Corinthian church may have been influenced by the social factors of Roman Corinth as shown by the evidences above. Their problems are resultant of the combined influence of their multi-ethnic composition, social status, patronage, and sophistic activities in the first century. In particular, the problems of division and boasting are occasioned by the special relationship that the patrons had with the missionary workers of the church. It is likely that these quarrels over their missionary workers are carried on with the leadership of the household patrons. That is, Paul is not only addressing the individual members of the congregations of the house churches but also primarily the patrons to cease from quarreling over their preferred missionary workers and rally their people to preserve the unity of the church. Likewise, the problem of wisdom is occasioned by the patrons' propensity to rhetoric. As a result, some of them viewed themselves as disciples of the eloquent Apollos while others especially those whom Paul baptized considered themselves as disciples of Paul. If it can be granted at this point, there is a high probability that the problems of division, boasting, and wisdom are led by the patrons whom Paul identifies in 1 Corinthians 1:26 and 4:10 as wise, powerful or strong, and noble or honorable along with the congregation in their respective house churches.

CHAPTER 3

Rhetorical Analysis of 1 Corinthians 1–4

In this chapter, I explore 1 Corinthians 1–4 using the steps of rhetorical criticism: analysis of the rhetorical unit, rhetorical situation, species of rhetoric, and the significance of Paul's arguments, structure, and style. Then I conclude by evaluating his rhetorical effectiveness and giving a summary analysis of his rhetorical arguments.

Further, the rhetorical analysis explains the nature and the relationship of the problems of division, boasting, and wisdom and how Paul addressed the three problems. It also demonstrates the identity of the groups who are quarreling.

3.1 The Rhetorical Unit

1 Corinthians 1–4 is a rhetorical unit where Paul seeks to persuade his audience to act upon an exigency. Every rhetorical unit has an opening, middle, and closing section. The opening section, 1 Corinthians 1:1–9, identifies the sender and the receiver. It also contains Paul's thanksgiving to God. 1 Corinthians 1:10–4:5 is the middle section that contains the body of Paul's message. It explains the rhetorical situation Paul addresses. It also explains Paul's admonition, recommendation, and appeal to the believers to act upon the exigencies in order to modify the situation. 1 Corinthians 4:6–21 is the closing section where Paul sets his final appeal to the believers to act upon the exigencies. Also, Paul exhorts the believers to imitate him and warns the arrogant people who are stirring division in the church.

3.2 The Rhetorical Situation

Here Paul is dealing with a complex rhetorical situation that has three interrelated exigencies.

3.2.1 The Exigencies in 1 Corinthians 1–4

As defined by Bitzer, exigence refers to a flawed reality which calls for an urgent intervention and modification.[1] There are three interrelated exigencies in this situation: the problem of division, the problem of boasting, and the problem of wisdom.

3.2.1.1 The Problem of Division

In 1 Corinthians there are three references to σχίσματα: 1:10, 11:18, and 12:25. The first two references indicate actual divisions in the church, whereas Paul uses 12:25 as part of his explanation on how the Holy Spirit distributes the gifts in the body of Christ.

In 1:10 Paul's appeal ἵνα τὸ αὐτὸ λέγητε πάντες suggests that Corinthian believers do not agree with one another. His reference to ἐν τῷ αὐτῷ νοῒ καὶ ἐν τῇ αὐτῇ γνώμῃ reinforces the idea that they are divided into groups and quarreling against each other. Paul describes their quarreling as the lack of unity of mind and intention. This is indicated by Paul's use of the word σχίσματα, which refers to the "condition of being divided because of conflicting aims or objectives."[2] The quarreling is probably related to the criticisms against Paul in 1 Corinthians 2:1–5 and the reference to being examined in 1 Corinthians 4:1–3. The meaning of the word ἔριδες in 1 Corinthians 1:11 is explained in 1:12 where Paul refers to the Corinthians being divided because of their conflicting opinions about their missionary workers – expressed by the claims Ἐγὼ μέν εἰμι Παύλου, Ἐγὼ δὲ Ἀπολλῶ, Ἐγὼ δὲ Κηφᾶ, Ἐγὼ δὲ Χριστοῦ in verse 12. The same quarreling is referred to in 1 Corinthians 3:3–4 where ἔρις is used alongside ζῆλος. According to BDAG, the quarreling involves "engagement in rivalry especially to positions taken in a matter, strife, discord, [and] contention."[3] The quarrels as described by the words ἔρις and

---

1. Bitzer, "Rhetorical Situation," 6.
2. BDAG, s.v. "σχίσμα."
3. BDAG, s.v. "ἔρις."

ζῆλος are causing a rift in relationships. The situation poses a serious threat to the unity of the church.

It is noted here that there is nothing in the text to suggest the names in the slogans are part of the quarrel. In fact, Paul affirms how God has used him and Apollos to do the work of God among the Corinthian believers. Paul's rebuke is directed towards the entire church, not to any group represented in the slogan. Margaret M. Mitchell remarks "Paul's rhetorical strategy is to combat the phenomenon of factionalism itself, not each individual faction directly."[4] If there is any hint that Paul expresses veiled hostility or polemic against any group or individual mentioned in the slogan, the closest we can find is an indirect tirade towards those who say "I am of Paul," where Paul says, "Was Paul crucified for you? Were you baptized in the name of Paul?"[5]

As mentioned in chapter 1, Munck argues that there are no factions but only cliques.[6] Isn't a clique also a kind of group? Mitchell observes that Munck's view suffers from what she calls a "definitional problem of what 'factionalism' is."[7] Thiselton's suggestion that the word σχίσματα in 1 Corinthians 1:10 is used "metaphorically to division of mind or judgment" tends to limit the division to an intellectual aspect.[8] That is, there are differences in opinion but no actual quarreling.

Gerd Luedemann proposes that probably the tension in the church was between Paul and the Cephas party. According to him, at the time of 1 Corinthians Paul and Cephas were not in agreement with each other due to the absence of any remark from Paul about the nature of their relationship, unlike the case of Apollos. In 1 Corinthians 3:6–9 Paul affirms his good relationship with Apollos when he speaks of him as his co-worker and their unity in Christ as the one who plants and the other who waters. However, in 3:10 Paul issues a warning on the one who builds. Taking 1 Corinthians 3:11 into consideration, Paul's veiled hostility against Cephas as the "rock" is evident when he says that Christ is the foundation. If Paul and Cephas's relationship had tension it follows that the Cephas party would be involved.

---

4. Mitchell, *Paul and the Rhetoric*, 67.

5. Mihaila, *Paul-Apollos Relationship*, 109–10; Pickett, *Cross in Corinth*, 49–50; Pogoloff, *Logos and Sophia*, 101–2.

6. Munck, *Paul*, 135–67. See also Munck, "Church without Factions," 61–70.

7. Mitchell, *Paul and the Rhetoric*, 70.

8. Thiselton, *First Corinthians*, 115–16.

However, Luedemann also concedes that it is difficult to establish this within 1 Corinthians 1–4. There are other references in 1 Corinthians where the arguments for this view are stronger but the evidence in 1 Corinthians 1–4 is the weakest of them.[9]

In relation to this, there are those who suggest that the tension exists between the group of those who follow Paul and the Apollos group. Niels Hyldahl notes that the arrival of Apollos had caused some troubles in the Corinthian church. The believers were attracted to him especially those with whom he ministered. Through his public ministry many became believers too and perhaps he even baptized some of them.[10] Raymond Pickett holds that the Apollos group is the most influential group, who are leading the criticisms against Paul. In response to the Apollos group Paul also criticizes them citing that their behavior reflects the behavior of those who are not spiritual people. He describes them as arrogant.[11] Joop Smit also suggests that Paul is concentrating his polemic against the Apollos group because Apollos's arrival (after Paul left Corinth) has affected how the Corinthian believers valuate him as indicated in 1 Corinthians 4:1–5. Like Paul, Apollos was also very bold in the proclamation of the gospel and refuted the Jews as indicated in Acts 18:27–28. Because of these things, some Corinthian believers started to boast about Apollos over Paul. So when Paul wrote to the church he particularly aimed his rebuke at those who follow Apollos, as indicated in 1 Corinthians 3:1–5 and 4:1–5. In fact, there is also a possibility that the use of the word ἀπολλυμένοις (perishing) in 1 Corinthians 1:18 and ἀπολλῶ (destroy) in 1:19 is intentional to allude to the "Apollonists," those who follow Apollos, and to Apollos himself.[12]

Similarly, Bradley J. Bitner hypothesizes that Paul's polemic in 1 Corinthians 3:1–5 is directed to Crispus whose social and religious influence as a synagogue ruler makes him the likely leader of the Apollos group (Acts 18:8). Bitner suggests that Crispus admired Apollos and became critical of Paul. In turn, Paul became indifferent to Crispus. Though he baptized Crispus and his household, Paul's indifference to Crispus seems apparent in

---

9. Luedemann, *Opposition to Paul*, 75–78.
10. Hyldahl, "Corinthian 'Parties,'" 19–32.
11. Pickett, *Cross in Corinth*, 59–60.
12. Smit, "What Is Apollos?," 241–44; Barton, "Some Influences," 207–23.

his epistolary conclusion in 1 Corinthians 16:15–18 where he commended Stephanus and his household but left out the name of Crispus.[13] Welborn proposes that Gaius along with Crispus are the two leading influencers in the Apollos group. That is, following the notion of Johannes Weis, Gaius and Crispus's names were not included in Paul's commendation in 1 Corinthians 16 because of their involvements in the factions not only as members but also probably as leading personalities of the Apollos group.[14]

Welborn not only supports the notion that the tension in the church exists between the Paul group and the Apollos group but also between Paul and Apollos. He claims that there are only two groups involved in the quarreling since he only referred to the Paul group and the Apollos group in 1 Corinthians 3:4. This indicates that Paul's polemic from 1 Corinthians 1:18–3:4 is directly addressed to the Apollos group who are criticizing him. Also, Paul's metaphor in 1 Corinthians 3:5–9 and his appeal in 4:6, where he specifically refers to himself and Apollos only, demonstrates that there are no other groups involved in the quarreling. Further, Welborn asserts that Paul's subtle attack against Apollos can be inferred from his statement about his commission as an apostle in 1 Corinthians 1:17 and his agricultural metaphor in 1 Corinthians 3:5–10. In 1 Corinthians 1:17, Paul asserts that God did not call him to baptize but to preach the gospel. This seems to be indirect attack to Apollos's reputation as a "baptizer" in Acts 18:25. In 1 Corinthians 3:5–10, Paul presents himself as someone of primary authority and status compared to Apollos as inferred from the statements "I planted, Apollos watered" and "like a master builder I laid the foundation but another one is building on it."[15] Robin Scroggs suggests that Paul and those who follow him are involved in the quarreling. The accusations against him signify that those who criticize him are attacking Paul and in return Paul tries to defend himself.[16]

I agree with Hyldahl, Pickett, Smit, Scroggs, Bitner, and Welborn who claim that those who criticize Paul are the Corinthian believers who prefer Apollos. However, to assume that Paul is involved in the quarreling (as suggested by Scroggs and Welborn) or Paul is particularly aiming his polemic

---

13. Bitner, *Paul's Political Strategy*, 267–71. Bitner's hypothesis explores three possible names which includes Erastus (Rom 16:23), Titius Justus (Acts 18:7), and Crispus (Acts 18:8).

14. Welborn, *End to Enmity*, 248–52.

15. Welborn, 372–76.

16. Scroggs, "Paul," 33–55.

against the followers of Apollos is not consistent with Paul's claims in at least four ways. First, Paul is writing to the entire church. There is no clear reference to any group in regard to his rebuke. Some portions of his message to the Corinthian believers in 1 Corinthians 1–4 might specifically address the behavior of a few people but the letter is written for the entire church in general.

Second, Paul claims that he and Apollos are co-workers in the work of God. In this case, how can Paul criticize Apollos and those who follow him? In fact, Paul calls Apollos "our brother" in 1 Corinthians 16:12. Smit's reading of the ἀπολλυμένοις (perishing) in 1 Corinthians 1:18 and ἀπολῶ (destroy) in 1:19 as a reference to the "Apollonists" has no clear exegetical and rhetorical basis. In addition, Bitner and Welborn's claim that the absence of commendations (from Paul) in 1 Corinthians 16 on Gaius and Crispus signifies that Paul's polemic is addressed to Apollos and the Apollos group needs to be read in light of the rhetorical function of Paul's commendation. Here, as part of his final rhetorical approach, Paul mentions the name of Stephanas because he was the bearer of the letter along with Fortunatus and Achaicus whom he is sending back to Corinth. Then, he appeals to the Corinthian brothers to submit to them. Here, Paul introduces his appeal with the phrase phrase παρακαλῶ δὲ ὑμᾶς similar to his appeal to imitate him in his *conquestio* in 1 Corinthians 4:16. Hence, there is no reference in 1 Corinthians 16 that may indicate that the absence of commendation implies Paul's indifference towards Gaius and Crispus. Similarly, it does not imply either that Paul is attacking Apollos and the Apollos group.

Third, instead of resolving the problems, he is making it worse if his polemic is aimed at Apollos and his party. This view contradicts his appeal earlier in 1:10 where he urges them to be in one mind. How can Paul call for unity of mind then attack Apollos and the Apollos group later in his letter? In addition, this interpretation contradicts the intent of a deliberative rhetoric.[17] Fourth, Paul claims to be their father and exhorts them to imitate him. If he is involved in the quarreling, how can they imitate him?

I argue that the division in the church is instigated by the quarrel between the Paul and Apollos groups because among the four names mentioned in the slogan, only the names of Paul and Apollos are repeated more than twice in 1 Corinthians 1–4 in relation to the problems of division and

---

17. See page 34.

boasting – specifically in 3:4–9 and especially when he asks in 3:4–5, "For when one says, 'I am of Paul,' and another says, 'I am of Apollos,' are you not mere men? What then is Apollos? And What is Paul?" and in 4:6 when he says, "Now these things brothers, I applied to myself and Apollos on your account in order that in us you may learn not to exceed what is written, in order that no one becomes arrogant on behalf of one against another." Although Cephas is mentioned again in 1 Corinthians 3:22 along with the names of Paul and Apollos, the purpose, however, is not to specifically refer to the group as part of the quarreling. The intention of mentioning those names functions more like a catalogue of names along with other matters such as "world," "life," and "death" in relation to belonging to Christ than a reference to the problems in the church. If there are Cephas and Christ groups, Paul could have at least connected them to the problems of division, boastings, and wisdom in 1 Corinthians 1–4. Thus, in this case, among the four names mentioned in the slogan only Paul and Apollos have a direct link to the problems in the Corinthian church, particularly the problems of division and boasting.

If the quarreling involves two major groups only, why did Paul mention the Cephas and Christ group? Paul's purpose of intentionally mentioning Cephas and Christ is an exaggeration to heighten the seriousness of the quarreling that is dividing the church into different groups. The names mentioned in the slogan are a catalogue of names to portray the gravity of the problems in the church.

3.2.1.2 The Problem of Boasting

The problem of boasting is the second exigency. In 1 Corinthians 1:12 Paul introduces the problem of boasting using anaphora in the phrases "I am of Paul," "I am of Apollos," "I am of Cephas," and "I am of Christ." In these phrases, the emphasis is not on the words "Paul," "Apollos," "Cephas," or "Christ" but on the word "I." Here, Paul is addressing not only their boasting of their preferred missionary worker but also about themselves (cf. 1 Cor 1:29, 31; 3:18, 21).[18]

After a long pause in his discussion about the boasting of the Corinthian believers, Paul resumes his criticism of their boastings in 1 Corinthians 3:1–9. Here Paul points out to the Corinthian believers that their jealousy

---

18. Cf. Munck, *Paul*, 150; Frestadius, "Spirit and Wisdom," 52–70.

and quarreling do not reflect the action of spiritual people. He asserts that there is no reason to boast about their leaders particularly about him and Apollos. There is no reason to quarrel about them because he and Apollos are co-workers in the work of the Lord. As co-workers they may have different roles but there is no quarrel or envy between them because they are doing the same work as servants of God. In 1 Corinthians 3:21 Paul concludes his admonition with a call to desist from boasting about their leaders.

In 1 Corinthians 4 Paul used a different word to describe this prideful attitude of the Corinthians. Here Paul discusses the theme of boasting using the two words καυχᾶσθαι and φυσιοῦσθαι. In 1 Corinthians 4:6 Paul refers to pride as being puffed up. In 1 Corinthians 4:1–6 Paul insists that they must not be regarded beyond who they really are. That is, they are servants of Christ whom God has entrusted with the mysteries God has revealed. In addition, the Corinthian believers must refrain from judging others including their leaders because only God knows the motives of the heart. In fact, Paul asserts that he does not even examine himself. This practice of examining one's self worth and the worth of others could lead someone to overestimate their worth and underestimate other's worth, which in effect leads to boasting about oneself and belittling others. This is exactly what is happening among those who are quarreling. It is in this light that the word φυσιοῦσθαι must be understood. That is, no one must regard themselves or other leaders beyond what or who they really are. Should any recognition be afforded it must come from God. According to BDAG φυσιοῦσθαι refers to an attitude where a person has an "exaggerated self-conception."[19] In 1 Corinthians 4:7 Paul continues the theme of boasting with the word καυχᾶσθαι again. Paul's usage of the two different terms is meant to highlight the degree of divisive attitudes that the Corinthian believers have. They do not only take pride only about their leaders, but also they have become conceited about who they are in relation to their leaders, which made them think they are superior to others.

Matthew R. Malcolm proposes that the core exigency in the church is the boastful attitude of the Corinthians believers. For him, boasting is not just one of the reasons of the conflicts in the church. Rather, the conflicts in the church are results of the boastful attitude of the Corinthians believers. His final contention is that boasting is theological, not factional, "because

---

19. BDAG, s.v. "φυσιόω."

it implied confidence outside of God, claiming in the present the manifest wisdom and spirituality that can only really be found hidden in Christ, awaiting manifestation at his future revelation."[20]

While I agree that boasting is a key factor in the quarrels in the church, Malcolm has failed to see the significance of how the three exigencies are connected to each other. To lump all three exigencies under the problem of boasting is not consistent with Paul's rhetorical structure and method. Paul's treatments of the problems show how each problem has contributed to the overall tension in the church. And because they are connected, he has interspersed his arguments in at least two key factors particularly the problem of boasting and wisdom in 1 Corinthians 1:18–31 and 3:18–21. Thus, further discussion of the nature of boasting is integrated in my discussion of the problem of wisdom below.

3.2.1.3 The Problem of Wisdom

The third exigency refers to the problem of wisdom in the church. When Paul called the attention of the Corinthian believers to the problem of division in the church, his discussion of the problem of division in 1 Corinthians 1:10–17 shifted to his teaching on wisdom in 1:18–2:16.

In 1 Corinthians 1:18–2:16 Paul argues that the wisdom of the world is futile for the following reasons. First, God has declared it doomed to destruction. Second, God has made it foolish. Notwithstanding its eloquence and knowledge, wisdom of the world failed to know God. In his superior wisdom God precludes the wisdom of the world from knowing him apart from God's self-revelation through Christ. It highlights not only God's sovereign choice to determine who can know him but also how he can be known. There is nothing the wisdom of the world can do to know God unless God wills it. Christ, the wisdom of God, is God's gift of salvation to those whom he called so that they might be righteous and holy. This means God does not qualify people by virtue of their social or political status but by God's sovereign choice to call them into his salvation even the least in society. God did this to shame the wisdom of the world and to show that no one has any reason to boast except in Christ. In addition, Paul explains the role of the Holy Spirit who reveals the mystery of God's wisdom, and that it is beyond the reach of

---

20. Malcolm, *Paul and the Rhetoric*, 155–57.

the wisdom of the world. Wisdom belongs to God and unless he reveals it through the Spirit to those whom he calls his own, and those who love him, wisdom cannot be known. The spiritual person is the one who understands the wisdom of God because the Spirit of God reveals it to them.

Thus, in 1 Corinthians 3:18–20 Paul cautions the Corinthian believers against the pitfall of thinking that they can be truly wise by pursuing the wisdom of the world. Instead, by reiterating his earlier arguments, Paul shows them the absurdity of pursuing the wisdom of the world. The Corinthian believers think they are wise but Paul refutes them by showing their claim is based on a false premise. That the wisdom of the world is foolishness before God is evident in the fact that it failed to know God or understand the wisdom of God in Christ.

Paul connects this to the problem of boasting. In 1 Corinthians 3:21 Paul echoes his earlier appeal in 1:10 after reiterating the futility of seeking the wisdom of the world because it is foolishness to God. This time Paul directly confronts their behavior by instructing them to desist from boasting about their leaders because what they perceive as superior wisdom is nothing but rubbish before God. It is absurd to boast and quarrel about their missionary workers. It is futile to let it cause division among them because none of them belong to their missionary workers. In fact, the opposite is true. No single missionary worker belongs to one group only. All their leaders belong to all of them. It follows that since they are in Christ all these things belong to Christ too. Consequently, since Christ belongs to God then these things belong to God. In a more aggressive tone in 1 Corinthians 4:7 Paul confronts their superior attitude also toward one another, their preferred missionary worker, and other missionary workers. The series of questions Paul asks are meant to make them realize how futile their perspectives are: "For who regards you as superior? What do you have that you did not receive? And if you did receive it, why do you boast as if you had not received it?" (4:7). The questions aim at addressing their false presumption of superiority and baseless boastings.

3.2.2 The Audience in 1 Corinthians 1–4

The second component of the rhetorical situation is the audience. Paul's audience is the whole Corinthian church. Paul wrote them because he heard from the household of Chloe that some members of the church are quarreling over their leaders (1 Cor 1:10–12). Though the Corinthian believers may have been passing judgment over Paul as indicated in 1 Corinthians 4:3–5, their relationship remains strong since they still wrote Paul to inquire about certain matters. Paul describes their father-children relationship in Christ in 4:14–16 where he even exhorts them to imitate him.

3.2.3 The Constraints in 1 Corinthians 1–4

The third component of the rhetorical situation is constraints. Constraints refer to people and their attitudes, beliefs, events, or relationships that increase the ability of the audience to respond accordingly to the desired action required in modifying the situation.[21]

The first constraint is the authority of Paul as an apostle who had been instrumental in the spreading of the gospel to Corinth. He is the spiritual father of the church (1 Cor 4:15). Through Paul's ministry they heard the gospel and believed in the Lord Jesus Christ. In fact, Paul baptized Crispus and Gaius in the church. His authority as their spiritual father makes the Corinthian believers well-disposed to pay attention to his arguments and follow the actions he recommends. The second constraint is the common faith Paul and the Corinthian believers share in Christ. In fact, Paul's call for the Corinthian believers to agree with one another is made based on the name of the Lord Jesus Christ. He made this appeal even before he started his arguments. The third constraint is the believers' commitment to the gospel of Christ. Paul built his rhetorical discourse around the gospel. He explains true wisdom to them in view of the gospel of Christ. The fourth constraint refers to the nature of Paul's preaching of the gospel. Paul reminds the Corinthian believers in 1 Corinthians 1:17 and 2:1–5 that his preaching of the gospel was not done according to the methods and principles of the wisdom of the world. Yet it was effective even though it was not achieved by relying on the use of persuasive words but through the power of the Spirit.

---

21. Bitzer, "Rhetorical Situation," 8.

3.3 Species of Rhetoric and Stasis Theory

According to Aristotle, there are three species of rhetoric: judicial, deliberative, and epideictic. As noted above, it is possible to find elements of the three species of rhetoric in a single rhetorical unit.[22]

3.3.1 Species of Rhetoric

Watson observes Paul usually employs a combination of species in a single rhetorical unit.[23] Quintilian notes deliberative and epideictic rhetoric complement each other. That is, whatever deliberative advises or admonishes, epideictic praises or blames.[24] In this case 1 Corinthians 1–4 is a combination of deliberative and epideictic rhetoric.

3.3.1.1 Deliberative Rhetoric

In 1 Corinthians 1–4 elements of deliberative rhetoric are expressed in Paul's persuasive advice regarding the quarrels in the church. Some members of the church have become puffed up about themselves in view of their missionary workers. As argued above, they boast about themselves and their preferred missionary workers because they have overestimated their worth as well as their missionary workers' worth. Paul devotes an extensive amount of space to persuading the Corinthian believers to change their attitude in relation to the quarreling, perception of themselves, and the missionary workers. In 1 Corinthians 1:10 he urges them to stop quarreling. In 1:18–2:5 Paul demonstrates that the wisdom of the world is inferior compared to the wisdom of God because it cannot know the wisdom of God unless the Spirit of God reveals it. He also rebukes them for their boasting about their missionary workers and shows them the right way, which is to boast in the Lord. In 3:1–23 Paul rebukes them for their fleshly attitude as evident in their jealousy and strife among them. Thus, he could not even give them solid teachings. In 3:18 he warns them about being deceived and instead calls on them to pursue wisdom according to the ways of the wisdom of God. In 4:5 he also instructs them to cease from passing judgment about other people. In 4:7 Paul also addresses the boastful attitude of the Corinthians who regard themselves as

---

22. Kennedy, *New Testament Interpretation*, 19; Watson, "Three Species of Rhetoric," 42.
23. Watson, "Three Species of Rhetoric," 42.
24. Quintilian, *Inst.* 3.7.28.

superior over others. He challenges their claim emphasizing that their claim has no basis at all. In a sense, he wants the Corinthian believers to change their hearts and pursue unity instead. In 4:16 he encourages them to imitate him. In 4:17 he urges them listen to Timothy whom he had sent to teach them in their walk with Christ.

3.3.1.2 Epideictic Rhetoric

In 1 Corinthians 1–4 elements of epideictic rhetoric are shown in Paul's praises and pronouncements regarding the inappropriate acts of the Corinthian believers. As a form of praise in 1:4 Paul expresses his thanksgiving to God for how the grace of God has been abundantly poured out to the Corinthian believers through the giving of the gifts needed for their life and ministry, which have continually confirmed the testimony of Christ in them.

In 1 Corinthians 1:18–2:5 Paul commends those who are being saved for taking the word of the cross as power of God as well as Christ as the power of God and wisdom of God. On the other hand, Paul denounces those who run after the wisdom of the world and who consider the word of the cross as foolishness. Paul also highlights the weakness of the wisdom of the world. It is inferior compared to the wisdom of God, emphasizing that the foolishness of God is even wiser than the wisdom of man. Paul also emphasizes that the Corinthian believers have nothing to boast about because when God called them, many of them were not wise, mighty, or noble.

In 1 Corinthians 3:1–23 Paul speaks highly of Apollos as his co-worker in the Lord whom God used to continually nurture them after Paul left Corinth. On the other hand, Paul calls them infants in Christ and "of the flesh" who could not take solid teachings and whose relationships are marred by jealousy and strife.

3.3.2 Stasis Theory

Stasis refers to the core question or accusation presented. It is here where the accusation is either negated or admitted by the one accused.[25] Although these kinds of stasis are applicable to all kinds of speeches (judicial, deliberative, and epideictic), stasis is oftentimes more applicable to judicial speeches.[26]

---

25. Peterson, *Eloquence*, 24.
26. Watson, *Invention*, 13.

Peterson suggests that the stasis of 1 Corinthians 1–4 is 4:1–5 where Paul exhorts the believers to regard them as servants of God. Paul also reminds them that only God has the authority to pass judgment on them at the proper time, that is, on the day the Lord returns. Thus, no one must pass judgment on one another.

It is not clear what the accusations and judgments are though. If indeed this section refers to an accusation or judgment, Paul is not even defending himself here. He is not negating or admitting anything. In fact, he even presents himself as a trustworthy servant of Christ and steward of the mysteries of God. In addition, Paul puts his integrity forward with the knowledge that it is the Lord who examines him.

In view of the lack of direct accusation against Paul and the fact that stasis is more applicable to judicial rhetoric, it is probable that 1 Corinthians 1–4 does not have a stasis since 1 Corinthians 1–4 is not a judicial rhetoric but a combination of deliberative and epideictic rhetoric.

3.4 Invention, Style, and Arrangement

For the purpose of this study, the analysis of the invention and style will be integrated in the analysis of arrangement. Arrangement refers to the structure of the rhetorical unit. The structure includes *exordium*, *narratio*, *partitio* or *propositio*, *probatio* (*probatio* also may include *refutatio*), and *peroratio*.[27]

3.4.1 The *Exordium*: 1 Corinthians 1:4–9

The *exordium* is the introductory statement of the author and it aims at preparing the audience to be attentive, open, well-disposed, and engaged to the speech.[28]

In 1 Corinthians 1:4–9 Paul sets the Corinthian believers to be receptive to his message by expressing his thanksgiving to God for the Corinthian believers. He also establishes how God has enriched them in speech and knowledge through Jesus Christ. This is an anticipation of Paul's discussion of wisdom in this rhetorical unit. Further, Paul raises their connection with Christ whom they bear witness in anticipation of Paul's treatment of the issue

---

27. Witherington, *Conflict and Community*, 44.
28. Quintilian, *Inst.* 4.1.5; Peterson, *Eloquence*, 24.

in 1 Corinthians 3 on how their lives reflect the character of Christ who has called them to be blameless.

This *exordium* though does not seem to introduce the topic that Paul wants to discuss below. Here Paul does not engage with the audience about the topic in order to excite them or disarm their objections and prejudices toward the topic he wants to present. Aristotle notes that there are times deliberative rhetoric may not have an *exordium* because oftentimes the audience is familiar with the subject matter already.[29]

3.4.2 The *Propositio*: 1 Corinthians 1:10

Partitio or *propositio* refers to presentation of the propositions the author wants to prove. It may also contain the proposition of the opponent.[30] *Partitio* or *propositio* also refers to the author's main thesis and advice.[31]

In 1 Corinthians 1:10 Paul presents his *propositio*, that is, the Corinthian believers must agree with one another so that there be no division in the church. The phrase τὸ αὐτὸ λέγητε does not mean they have to say the same words or agree to have the same slogan. It does not mean too that they always must think similarly in all issues.[32] Rather it means they reach the point of agreeing with one another by having the same mind and intention. Mitchell says the phrase τὸ αὐτὸ λέγητε is used to "describe the opposite of factionalism. Those who 'say the same thing' are allies, compatriots, even co-partisans. Simply put, they agree with one another."[33] As discussed above in the problem of division, people are divided into groups because they have conflicting opinions about their missionary workers which is expressed in the phrases Ἐγὼ μέν εἰμι Παύλου, Ἐγὼ δὲ Ἀπολλῶ, Ἐγὼ δὲ Κηφᾶ, Ἐγὼ δὲ Χριστοῦ. Thus, Paul's appeal is aimed at restoring the relationships that have been ripped apart because of their quarrels.[34] As an apostle of the Lord Jesus Christ and the founding minister of the Corinthian church Paul could have exercised his apostolic authority by demanding the church to stop quarreling and unite. Yet he chooses to persuade them through an appeal for unity. His appeal

---

29. Aristotle, *Rhet.* 3.14.1415b.12.
30. Watson, *Invention*, 21.
31. Kennedy, *New Testament Interpretation*, 24.
32. Cf. Polhill, "Wisdom of God," 325–39.
33. Mitchell, *Paul and the Rhetoric*, 68.
34. Cf. Mitchell, 74–75.

stands not only on logic but also anchors on the nature of his relationship with his audience, an essential element in effective persuasion. First, he appeals for unity based on his personal relationships with them as an apostle of the Lord Jesus Christ indicated by his use of the term "brothers." Second, Paul appeals for unity based on the authority of the name of the Lord Jesus Christ with whom they are called into fellowship. That is, their unity is not based on any human reason but based in the name of the Lord Jesus Christ. Thus, they must not let anything to destroy their unity as a church. G. J. Steyn writes, "When this is seen against the background of the baptism formula which was pronounced loud and clear during their baptism the appeal to the ὄνομα τοῦ κυρίου as the one Name standing out above all the rest, is an indirect condemnation of the various party names."[35]

3.4.3 The *Narratio*: 1 Corinthians 1:11–17

Kennedy hints that although deliberative rhetoric does not necessarily require a *narratio*, it may be placed after the *propositio* to describe the reasons and facts of the *propositio* before proving the case as well as refuting the point of view of the audience.[36]

1 Corinthians 1:11–17 serves as the *narratio* in 1 Corinthians 1–4. Paul explains how the news reached him through the household of Chloe. There are two possible reasons why Paul must inform them how the news reached him. First, Paul probably wants to make it clear that it was not Stephanas, Fortunatus, and Achaicus who brought the news to him. The Corinthian church sent these men to deliver the official letter to Paul to ask him on matters affecting the situation in the church. Second, it is interesting to note the Corinthian believers did not include this matter in their official letter to Paul. It seems they did not consider the current quarreling in the church worthy of their attention or Paul's intervention, an example of a mean case where the audience deems the situation or topic trivial.[37] Hurd alludes to the possibility that perhaps they did not want Paul to know about the situation or respond

---

35. Steyn, "Reflections," 484–85.
36. Kennedy, *New Testament Interpretation*, 24.
37. Identifying the kind of case is usually done in the *exordium* part but since Paul's letter does not have an appropriate *exordium* for a deliberative rhetoric, Paul introduces it here as part of *narratio*. Cf. Bitzer, "Rhetorical Situation," 7.

to it.[38] However, Paul perceives the damage this situation may bring to the church if the situation is ignored continually. Paul disarms the justifications of their quarrels by showing that the current situation of the church does not reflect their identity in Christ.

Earlier Paul mentioned the Corinthian believers are sanctified in Christ and saints in calling as well as called into fellowship with Jesus Christ (1 Cor 1:2–9). Here Paul alludes to their identity and fellowship with Christ. In 1:13 through series of rhetorical questions Paul emphasizes that as people who are in Christ, they are supposed to be in good fellowship with one another. Paul asks, "Has Christ been divided? Paul was not crucified for you, was he? Or were you baptized in the name of Paul?" Certainly, Christ is not divided so there is no reason to allow any cause to divide the fellowship of the members of the body of Christ. Certainly, Paul was not crucified for them and they were not baptized in the name of Paul or any of the missionary workers so there is no reason to favor one over the other or to appropriate loyalty to one at the expense of another missionary worker. It seems Paul is alluding to baptism as one of the possible causes of the quarrels (who baptized who).

Paul expresses his delight that he did not baptize any of them except Crispus and Gaius (and probably their respective household), which seems to indicate that he was glad he couldn't be made accessory to how this quarreling has evolved over time. Then Paul clarifies that God did not call him to baptize but to preach the gospel. John William Beaudean Jr. notes that when Paul said baptism is not his "apostolic commission" he was actually emphasizing "he finds no justification for their divisions."[39] As such it is pointless to put value on baptism over the preaching of the gospel. In fact, the questions he asked paint an absurd image of the cause of their quarreling. But the absurdity of the image he presents makes the rebuke more intense. At this point, it seems that Paul uses the subject of baptism to realign the attention of the Corinthians from their quarrels to Christ. The discussion is aimed at refocusing the people from their missionary workers to Christ, the one who sent these missionary workers to Corinth.

In 1:17 Paul transitions to the *probatio* where he discusses the issue more deeply. The phrase οὐκ ἐν σοφίᾳ λόγου refers to the manner of speaking that

---

38. Hurd, *Origin*, 75–76.
39. Beaudean, *Paul's Theology*, 91–93.

is closely identified with human ability to make an act of proclamation. It is translated "cleverness in speaking."[40] In this context the speaker convinces the audience to agree with his proposed solution to the exigency at hand. Thus, success in speaking is based on the speaker's persuasiveness. So, when Paul says he did not rely on the use of human persuasiveness as was the popular manner of public speaking, Paul seems to distinguish himself from the reason of the quarrels where people are saying Ἐγὼ μέν εἰμι Παύλου, Ἐγὼ δὲ Ἀπολλῶ, Ἐγὼ δὲ Κηφᾶ, Ἐγὼ δὲ Χριστοῦ. Paul wants them to understand that they should put an end to their sloganeering, not even those who say "I am for Paul" because he couldn't be categorized with these other preachers due to the fact that God sent him to preach the gospel not with wisdom of words. Also, Paul's statement about the manner of his preaching elucidates Paul's conviction about his calling as a preacher of the gospel. The emphasis of the phrase "not with wisdom of words" is on how God wants him to preach. God did not send him to preach the gospel relying on human persuasion to convince his audience because the gospel is the power of God as indicated by Paul in 1 Corinthians 1:18. In fact, this can be explained more clearly when we compare 1:17 with 2:1–5. Both passages point to each other. Comparing these verses clarify not only the manner of preaching by which God wants him to accomplish it but also its impact on the listeners. Paul underlines that in view of his conviction about his calling as a preacher of the gospel, he made the conscious choice to proclaim the message not according to human persuasiveness so that the hearers will respond to the content of his message through the power of God. To this effect, the credit goes to Christ and not to him as the preacher. Paul is firm in his conviction that the task of preaching the gospel is a divine work and must be conducted that way all the time. Otherwise, the "cross' own power to create belief" shall be voided.[41] Elizabeth Castelli explains, "The emphasis here is on Paul's 'contentless' nature; he is simply a conduit through which the gospel passes . . . He is the one who is supposed to speak while it is not he who speaks at all, but Christ through him."[42]

---

40. BDAG, s.v. "σοφός."
41. Litfin, *St. Paul's Theology*, 189–92.
42. Castelli, *Imitating Paul*, 99.

3.4.4 The *Probatio*: 1 Corinthians 1:18–4:5

The *probatio* refers to the presentation of proof to prove the case of the author against his audience. Here, we find Paul using both internal and external proofs. Further, in deliberative rhetoric a *probatio* states the reasons for the readers to follow "the course of action that is being advised" with a vision of how their obedience would benefit them in the future.[43] *Probatio* may also include *refutatio* of the arguments of the opponent or the audience.

In 1 Corinthians 1:18–4:13 Paul elaborates his *probatio*. He demonstrates that the problem they are facing is a multi-layered problem that takes its roots from their improper understanding of wisdom resulting in boasting and causing division in the church. In this section we can also find *refutatio* where Paul demolishes their assumptions on wisdom and condemns their boastings. In his *refutatio* Paul explains true wisdom and shows them how they are supposed to live as people of God according to the wisdom of God and the power of God.

Internal proof refers to the argumentation developed by the speaker to support their claims or accusation. There are three kinds of internal proof: *ethos*, *pathos*, and *logos*. In *ethos* the speaker attempts to convince their audience by establishing their integrity and demonstrates that they possess the authority based on their character. As a result, the audience can trust their judgments regarding what is beneficial or harmful.[44] Paul enumerates his credibility in the following ways: (1) in 1 Corinthians 1:2 he says that his apostleship is not by human standards but by the will of God; (2) in 1:10–17 he calls them brothers and claims to have baptized a few of them; (3) in 1:18 he identifies himself along with the Corinthian believers as those who belong to the ones being saved; (4) in 3:9 he calls Apollos and other leaders his co-workers in the Lord; (5) in 3:10 he reminds them that he laid the foundation for the ministry at Corinth; (6) in 4:1–5, he presents his trustworthiness as a servant of Christ and steward of the mysteries of God; and (7) in 4:15 he calls them his children to assert his authority as their father in Christ through the gospel.

In *pathos* the speaker stirs the emotions of the audience to direct them to the action they want them to do. In this rhetorical unit Paul begins by

---
43. Witherington, *Conflict and Community*, 106.
44. Quintilian, *Inst.* 3.8.13.

challenging the wise man, the scribe, and the debater. He attacks the wisdom of the world, declares God's judgment upon it and calls it inferior when compared to the wisdom of God (1 Cor 1:18–25). Then, he reminds them of their low social status and highlights the greatness of God's wisdom when he chose them in their lowly state and counsels them not to boast anymore (1 Cor 1:26–31). In 1 Corinthians 3, however, Paul directly confronts them again. In 3:1–4 he calls them infants in Christ and fleshly. He instructs them they are the temple of God whom the Spirit of God has dwelled within and warns them of God's judgment if they don't take care of it (1 Cor 3:16–17). He counsels them not to be deceived into thinking that they have already reached the pinnacle of spirituality (1 Cor 3:18). In 1 Corinthians 4 he advises them to regard their leaders as co-workers in Christ and commands them to cease from passing judgment about them (1 Cor 4:1–5). Through rhetorical questions and using irony, Paul paints a stark contrast between the Corinthians and their situation to condemn their false sense of superiority underscoring that what they have are things they have received from others and to accentuate that their boastings are divisive. Paul calls them as people who are already filled, have become rich, and kings without the help of the church leaders. He cites them as prudent, strong, and distinguished while he and the rest of the leaders are fools, weak, and without honor (1 Cor 4:7–13).[45] Finally he warns those who have become arrogant that he would deal them either harshly or gently when he visits them (1 Cor 4:18–21).

In *logos* the speaker presents his arguments using *induction* and *deduction*. As discussed in chapter 1, Aristotle suggests induction is more appropriate for deliberative rhetoric, deduction for judicial rhetoric, and since there is no dispute involved in epideictic rhetoric, amplification is more suitable to it.[46] Induction refers to the process of asking questions using argument by analogy (questions that build on each other) in order to lead the audience to agree to the view or action proposed by the speaker. In 1 Corinthians 1:18–2:16 Paul employs the argument by definition (an example of *logos*) to explain the meaning of the wisdom of God to the Corinthians believers to establish that they have wrongly understood true wisdom. This is where

---

45. Cf. Holland, "Paul's Use of Irony," 234–48.
46. Aristotle, *Rhet.* 1.9.1368a.40.

Paul begins to refute their wisdom concept by showing them it is fallacious and a futile pursuit.

In 1:20–25 Paul challenges the wise man, the scribe, and the debater. Through the use of argument by analogy and anaphora (through the repeated use of the phrase "where is the") Paul strengthens his argument to point out that not only the wisdom of the world has been judged by God but also it has been rendered incapable of understanding the wisdom of God: "Where is the wise man? Where is the scribe? Where is the debater of this age? Has not God made foolish the wisdom of the world?"[47] Here, Paul shows that if the wise man, scribe, and the debater of this age could not understand the wisdom of God through the wisdom of the world, then who else could understand it? Conzelmann observes that Paul declared the judgment of God upon the wisdom of the world "is passed, in the form of a question, not by reasoning, but by asserting the act of God."[48]

External proof refers to documents or witnesses that a speaker presents to support his claim or accusation. In the New Testament, common external proofs are "quotations of Scripture, the evidence of miracles, and the naming of witnesses."[49]

Concerning the division in the church Paul mentions that the quarreling among the believers is threatening the unity of the church, which he learned through the household of Chloe. Regarding his discussion of wisdom at 1 Corinthians 1:19 Paul gives an Old Testament citation from the book of Isaiah where God declares his eschatological judgment on the wisdom of the world. Using Isaiah 29:14 Paul reminds the Corinthians there is no point of arguing further on this issue because God has already made up his mind and has spoken already about the futility of the wisdom of the wise. This establishes the futility of their wisdom pursuit as well. John Barclay concurs with this when he notes that Paul is not just contrasting between the wisdom of God and the wisdom of the world but he uses it to "announce a divine intention to *overturn or destroy* the wisdom that is not God's own."[50] That God is able to destroy the wisdom of the wise, "the highest form of wisdom,

---

47. Cf. Fitzmyer, *First Corinthians*, 152.
48. Conzelmann, *1 Corinthians*, 43.
49. Kennedy, *New Testament Interpretation*, 14.
50. Barclay, "Crucifixion as Wisdom," 1–20. Cf. Williams, *Wisdom of the Wise*, 89–90.

the wisdom of those deemed to be the wise 'ones,'" and the cleverness of the clever, the "very intelligence upon which the intelligent rely for their high status in the world" sets the wisdom of God above the wisdom of the world.[51] Thus, Paul can say, "Where is the wise? Where is the scribe? Where is the debater of this world? Has not God made foolish the wisdom of the world?"

In 1 Corinthians 1:31 Paul cites Jeremiah 9:22–23 (LXX) to address the boasting of the Corinthian believers. In the preceding verses Paul disarms them from having any ground to boast by establishing that none of them participated in their salvation because everything was God's work. In addition, Paul also refutes any form of human boasting based on human accomplishments or merit. He brings his argument to its climax by emphasizing that the only legitimate way to boast is to boast in the Lord. That is, in light of the salvation they received from God through Christ the appropriate way of boasting is to boast about what God has done for them rather than boast on what they accomplished. John Paul Heil suggests two ways of understanding this phrase in light of the previous verses. First, boasting in the Lord may mean trusting in God who chose and called them in Christ, and trusting in Christ "who became for us wisdom from God, righteousness and sanctification and redemption" (1 Cor 1:30). Second, this statement also sets the legitimate object as well as reason of boasting especially in relation to 1 Corinthians 3:21. That is, no one is to boast in human beings but in God alone.[52]

1 Corinthians 2:6–16 presents two external proofs where Paul emphasizes that this wisdom of God is the kind of wisdom that cannot be discerned based on human understanding unless God reveals it. Paul explains the role of the Spirit of God in the revelation of wisdom and why people cannot understand the wisdom of God. Again, Paul exposes the limitation of the wisdom of the world in knowing the wisdom of God. This is the reason why in 2:8 the rulers of the age crucified Christ. They did not understand the plan of God that Christ is God's agent for the salvation of humanity. This is where Paul continues to disarm the wisdom of the world. They claim to possess wisdom yet they cannot understand the plan of God. Thus, in 2:9 Paul refers to an

---

51. Heil, *Rhetorical Role*, 20–22.
52. Heil, 41–46. Cf. Williams, *Wisdom of the Wise*, 129–32.

external proof again where he quotes from Isaiah 64:4 to conclude his argument in light of what he has written in verses 6–8.[53]

This is where Paul makes his point as he highlights the role of the Spirit in the revelation. That is, without the Spirit human beings cannot understand the wisdom of God. Paul says these things are beyond the reach of the wisdom of the world. It belongs to God and unless God reveals it through the Spirit it cannot be known. God has revealed it through the Holy Spirit to those he calls his own, to those who love him. Thus, in 1 Corinthians 2:16 Paul quotes from Isaiah 40:13 to conclude his argument by saying that the person without the Spirit cannot understand the things from God. Such a person cannot understand the wisdom of God so he is not truly wise or spiritual. Hence, he cannot also pass judgment on the πνευματικὸς who has the mind of Christ. The πνευματικὸς is the one understands the wisdom of God because the Spirit of God reveals it to him. It is also possible that this statement bears a double intent where in view of 1 Corinthians 2:15b Paul may be telling the Corinthian believers that they have no capacity and right to examine him.

In 1 Corinthians 3:19 and 20 Paul appeals to Old Testament texts from Job 5:12–13 and Psalm 94:11 (LXX 93:11) to emphasize the foolishness of pursuing wisdom of the world and avoid being deceived into thinking that they can become wise by pursuing it. Following the thread of argument, it also reiterates the futility of boasting in men or their leaders. This recalls his earlier discussion in 1 Corinthians 1:17 and 1:18—2:5 about the futility of the wisdom of the world. In 1:18 Paul mentions that the message of the cross is foolishness to those who are perishing. Here Paul confronts it with finality by declaring that the wisdom of the world is foolishness in the sight of God. Paul uses these texts to seal his argument on the superiority of God over the wisdom of the world. The wisdom of the world cannot outwit the wisdom of God. It is foolishness in the sight of God, who knows their reasoning is futile. As Fee puts it, "The ultimate irony is that people are cunningly avoiding the God with whom they have to do; but God has used that very cunning to ensnare them. Thinking themselves to be wise, they are in fact fools."[54] Here

---

53. Cf. Barrett, *Commentary on the First Epistle*, 73; Williams, *Wisdom of the Wise*, 201–2.
54. Fee, *First Epistle*, 152. Cf. Williams, *Wisdom of the Wise*, 326–30.

we can also find that Paul's style of discussing the *probatio* includes the use of antithesis, anaphora, and rhetorical questions.[55]

In 1 Corinthians 1:18, using antithesis, Paul demonstrates two contrasting viewpoints on the word of the cross between those who are perishing and those who are being saved. The former considers the word of the cross as foolishness and the latter considers it as power of God. What does Ὁ λόγος γὰρ ὁ τοῦ σταυροῦ mean? As will be seen below, the proclamation of the cross also refers to the content, Christ crucified, who is the power of God and the wisdom of God. Thus, in this context the phrase Ὁ λόγος γὰρ ὁ τοῦ σταυροῦ refers both to the act of the proclamation and the content of proclamation.[56] In Paul's view the cross draws two different responses from the hearers: foolishness to those who are perishing but power of God to those who are being saved.

In 1 Corinthians 1:22–24 Paul highlights the antithetical responses about the wisdom of God where it is a stumbling block to the Jews and foolishness to the Gentiles but to those whom God has called Christ is the power of God and wisdom of God. Here Paul underscores the failure of the wisdom of the world to understand the wisdom of God apart from God's revelation. That is, only those who are in Christ can understand the wisdom of God.

In 1 Corinthians 1:26–31 Paul continues to emphasize his argument that the wisdom of the world cannot know God apart from Christ. Through the use of anaphora where the phrases "not many" and "God chose" are repeated three times, Paul reminds the believers about their status when God called them and emphasizes that God chose them on the basis of his sovereign decision not on their human qualification.

Further in 1 Corinthians 2:1–5 Paul shows the antithetical ways that the gospel was preached to them. Paul recalls his earlier statement in 1 Corinthians 1:17 where he emphasized that God sent him to preach the gospel and not with wisdom of words. Paul cites that he came in weakness, fear, and much trembling. By portraying himself as a preacher who came in weakness, fear, and much trembling, he presents himself in a totally different manner in contrast to the rhetors of his time.[57] Paul says they received the

---

55. Kennedy, *New Testament Interpretation*, 25–26.
56. Cf. Barbour, "Wisdom and the Cross," 57–71.
57. Lim, "Not in Persuasive Words," 137–49.

gospel not on the basis of the persuasive nature of his preaching but through the demonstration of the power of God. Their conversion is proof that it was not accomplished through the external demonstration of rhetorical prowess but through the internal conviction of the Spirit.

In 1 Corinthians 3:1–5 Paul calls them infants in Christ. In 3:4–5, using an argument by analogy to depict how antithetical their claim and their actions are, he asks, "For since there is jealousy and strife among you, are you not fleshly, and are you not walking like mere men? For when one says, 'I am of Paul,' and another, 'I am of Apollos,' are you not *mere* men? What then is Apollos? And what is Paul?" Their jealousy, strife, and boastings are incompatible with the deeds of spiritual people.

In 1 Corinthians 3:6–17 Paul also uses metaphor to show how he and Apollos fit in the whole picture of God's overall work in their lives. That is, both of them are just servants of God. They should not be pitted against each other because they are doing the same work and preaching the same gospel. More importantly the believers should not quarrel over them especially in relation to their achievements as servants of God because whatever results they have seen from their works are things caused by God. None of them deserves any glory or loyalty for everything is God's work. Paul also explains they fulfilled their roles not based on worldly foundation but on Christ, the true foundation.

Paul's claim, that he and Apollos are co-workers in the work of the Lord, has some implications for his earlier statement about the nature of the preaching of the gospel. In 1 Corinthians 1:17 and 2:4–5 Paul asserts that God did not send him to preach the gospel using human persuasion but with the power of God. Since Paul and Apollos are both servants of God whom God has tasked to preach the same message in the same manner then it follows that though Apollos was known to be an eloquent preacher, he did not preach the gospel using human persuasion but with God's power as well.

In 1 Corinthians 3:16 through a rhetorical question Paul conveys they are temple of God who are called to live holy lives.

In 1 Corinthians 3:18–23, by way of argument by repetition, Paul continues to emphasize that their wisdom pursuit is futile. Considering what has been established above that Christ crucified is the wisdom of God, no one must be deceived into thinking they can be wise according to the standards of the world by pursuing the wisdom of the world. One must embrace the message of the cross and believe in the Christ crucified, a thing considered by the world as foolishness, so that they may be wise. Thus, one must become fool first so they may be wise. In addition, a contrast in 1:18–25 is reiterated here. The wisdom of the world considers the wisdom of God foolishness. In contrast, God considers the wisdom of the world foolishness too.

In 1 Corinthians 4:1–5 where Paul picks up his argument from the end of 1 Corinthians 3, he continues to assert that he and Apollos must be treated as co-workers, servants of God, stewards of the mysteries of God, and people who belong to God just as everyone is. There is no need to boast about anyone of them.

More importantly, Paul concludes his *probatio* by appealing on the basis of his trustworthiness as a servant of Christ and steward of the mysteries of God. He presents his *ethos*. This is an important element in the *probatio* where the rhetor establishes their integrity to show to their audience that they are trustworthy as well as their message so that the listeners will be moved to act upon the exigency. In addition, Paul's awareness of his trustworthiness is made with the knowledge that the one who called him to be his servant and steward of the mysteries of God is the one examines him. This explains why he sees no need to examine himself.

Shaping his argument in light of the coming of the Lord Jesus Christ Paul urges the Corinthian believers not to judge others because at the proper time when the Lord returns, he shall be the one to judge. Such judgment will be carried out not based on their social status or eloquence but on the condition and motives of their hearts. F. W. Grosheide notes that in the context of Paul's discussion on boastings Paul's exhortation means that he forbids the Corinthians to judge their leaders because only the Lord can judge the leaders whether they have been trustworthy servants of Christ and stewards of the mysteries of God.[58] Paul does not want the believers to judge others or him because this practice may lead them to either look down on others or boast on another. As such, either action may lead to boasting about one oneself or another person. In addition, as a closing appeal in his *probatio* Paul exhorts the Corinthian believers not to judge others because their critical spirit is detrimental to the unity of the church. This is the reason why there are quarrels and boasting among them.

---

58. Grosheide, *First Epistle to the Corinthians*, 101.

3.4.5 The *Peroratio*: 1 Corinthians 4:6–21

1 Corinthians 4:6–21 serves as the *peroratio* for 1 Corinthians 1–4. *Peroratio* is the final emotional summary appeal in view of the *probatio* where the author seeks to stir the emotions of the audience to favorably respond to the author's point of view and heed the actions required to modify the situation.[59] To achieve their goal in the *peroratio*, the author usually employs the amplification method either by inspiring, instigating anger, or appealing for compassion.[60] *Peroratio* has three parts: summing up, *indignatio*, and *conquestio*.[61]

In summing up, Paul reiterates his argument that there is no reason to boast about their leaders because their leaders stand equal in Christ and have been called to become servants of Christ and stewards of the mysteries of God. He urges the believers to stop boasting about him and Apollos because it is causing division in the church (1 Cor 4:6). The argument of this section indicates that to better understand the phrase "not to go beyond what is written," it must be interpreted in light of 4:16 where Paul appeals to the Corinthian believers to imitate him.[62] Here Paul emphasizes that the believers must learn from his and Apollos's example. That is, in view of 1 Corinthians 3:6–4:5, they serve God with the same mind and intention. Their primary agenda is to fulfill the task God has assigned each and not outrank or outshine each other. He and Apollos may have different roles but they are not in competition or jealous of each other. Rather, they work as servants of God. Thus, the Corinthian believers must follow their example by refraining from boasting about them.[63]

However, in *indignatio* Paul provokes the Corinthian believers by challenging their claim of superiority. Through rhetorical questions Paul demolishes their claim of superiority by alluding to the idea that who they claim to be is unwarranted. He also wants them to concede that their boasting is unsubstantiated. Paul writes in 4:7, "For who regards you as superior? What do you have that you did not receive? And if you did receive it, why do you boast as if you had not received it?" In 4:8–13 through amplification by enlarging

---

59. Witherington, *Conflict and Community*, 44.
60. Watson, *Invention*, 26–28.
61. Cicero, *Inv.* 1.52.98.
62. Pickett, *Cross in Corinth*, 79–80.
63. Castelli, *Imitating Paul*, 105–6; cf. Hooker, "Beyond," 127–32.

Paul describes the Corinthian believers as people who are already filled, have become rich, and kings without the help of Paul and other teachers. On the other hand, using amplification by reducing Paul speaks of himself and other teachers as fools, weak, and without honor in contrast to the Corinthian believers who are prudent, strong, and distinguished. This is not an admission of weakness but part of a rhetorical strategy where Paul uses irony or sarcasm to confront their false sense of superiority.

In the *conquestio*, Paul clarifies his intentions in writing to them, not to shame but to admonish them (1 Cor 4:14–21). He reminds them too about the foundation and nature of their relationship, that is, in Christ he has become their "father" through the gospel. In 4:16, he exhorts them as his children to imitate him (their father in Christ through the gospel). This verse marks the closing of the loop of Paul's arguments which is marked using παρακαλῶ.[64] In 1 Corinthians 1:10 he opens his arguments with an appeal to agree with one another in Christ: παρακαλῶ δὲ ὑμᾶς, ἀδελφοί. Here in 4:16 he closes it with an appeal to imitate him: παρακαλῶ οὖν ὑμᾶς. Dahl takes this final appeal as an appeal for loyalty to Paul. As noted in chapter 1, Dahl asserts that the Corinthians believers are questioning Paul's apostolic authority. So, the phrase παρακαλῶ οὖν ὑμᾶς is an appeal to be with one accord with him.[65] However, the context does not explicitly support both notions. It cannot be clearly established that Paul's authority is in question and since this first notion is ambiguous, then the second cannot stand. In addition, nothing in the immediate context hints the second notion. Rather, as will be discussed below, the appeal points to the fact that Paul wants the believers to imitate him so that the exigencies can be appropriately resolved. Mitchell notes, "The consistent rhetorical strategy of the letter is an appeal to Paul himself as the exemplar of loving, sacrificial concession for the greater good – unity and peace – whom he calls upon *all* Corinthians to emulate."[66]

Another interesting note in Paul's approach is that in his opening appeal he calls them his brothers while in his final appeal he calls them his children. This approach underscores both his apostolic and spiritual authority over them as one who has helped establish the church which further affirms

---

64. Barnett, *Corinthian Question*, 85.
65. Dahl, "Paul and the Church," 319.
66. Mitchell, "Corinthian Correspondence," 17–54.

that his authority is not in question here. Trevor Burke offers an interesting analysis of the familial metaphor that Paul uses in his closing arguments. According to Burke, Paul's final appeal demonstrates his spiritual authority as their "father" to call them to unite. Paul asserts that among those who have come to visit to Corinth and taught them about their Scripture he stands as their "principal father in the gospel" (1 Cor 4:15). Burke points out five key aspects of the social expectations of the father-child relationship in the ancient world that helps provide better appreciation of Paul's use of the paternal imagery: hierarchy, authority, imitation, affection, and education. First, fathers are expected to establish hierarchy in the family and govern his family well. Children, likewise, are expected to honor their parents particularly their father. Second, fathers are expected to demonstrate authority over the family. This is closely associated with the concept of hierarchy. This means they must exercise hierarchical, not tyrannical authority. They should not be harsh towards their children. Children are expected to obey their parents particularly their father. Third, fathers are expected to live an exemplary life of good conduct and behavior for their children to imitate. Fourth, though love is reciprocal, fathers must love their children more than their children love them. Fifth, fathers must train their children and provide them with good education. In anchoring his exhortation to the Corinthian believers to imitate him, Paul seems to adopt the paternal imagery of the ancient world "who was responsible in exercising authority as well as maintaining order, peace and concord within his family."[67] Now we ask the question, imitate him on what?

There are at least two possible ways of considering Paul's final appeal. The first approach is to consider this command in view of the missionary life and leadership of Paul. Generally, as a missionary Paul had gone through life being threatened and humiliated. He encountered difficult circumstances, troubles, and sufferings. He had been rejected, criticized, mocked, persecuted, and judged by other people. The description of the life of a missionary in 1 Corinthians 4:9–13 illustrates not only the dangers and troubles in life Paul had faced but also the challenges of responding in a manner that demonstrates the ways of Christ to people who were not loving to them and situations that

---

67. Burke, "Paul's Role," 107. Cf. Ehrensperger, *Paul*, 144–49; Fiorenza, "Rhetorical Situation," 386–403.

were not favorable to them.⁶⁸ The second approach is to consider this in view of the context of 1 Corinthians 1–4. Particularly, in this section where Paul gives his *conquestio* as explained above he appeals to them as their father. This metaphor sets the atmosphere of obedience for the children to obey and more importantly, imitate their father.⁶⁹

In 1 Corinthians 3 Paul explains his relationship with Apollos in view of the quarreling, jealousy, and boasting of the believers. In the same manner that he maintains a harmonious relationship with Apollos as his fellow worker in the work of God he exhorts the Corinthian believers to imitate him.⁷⁰ Kathy Ehrensperger further explains that Paul's exhortation to imitate him offers a visible illustration on how they can be united notwithstanding the divergent opinions they may have about their leaders. It is Paul's final attempt to urge the Corinthian believers to modify their deplorable situation. Ehrensperger writes,

> Paul actually sets the relationship of Apollos and himself as the example to be imitated when it comes to dealing with differing groups within the community. He does not deny or rule out the existence of difference, but acknowledges it positively. Yet he rules out quite clearly any option for boasting, that is, an attitude of dominance and triumph over others. He does not set himself as an example to be imitated like an isolated authoritarian ruler whom they should obey, but what is to be imitated here is a relationship between people who are and remain different.⁷¹

Both approaches are possible when it is viewed in light of the exigencies Paul is addressing. The first approach shows that even in the most difficult situation especially in relation to what Paul said above that he does not judge or examine others because judging others is detrimental to the unity of the church, like what is happening in the church at present. In the same manner, when they are not treated fairly by others like Paul they can say "when we are reviled, we bless; when we are persecuted, we endure; when we are slandered, we try to conciliate" (1 Cor 4:12–13). The second approach points

---

68. Plummer, "Imitation of Paul," 219–35.
69. Sanders, "Imitating Paul," 353–63. Cf. Burke, "Paul's Role," 107–10.
70. Burke, "Paul's Role," 105–11.
71. Ehrensperger, *Paul*, 149. Cf. Pickett, *Cross in Corinth*, 59.

to a more specific application of imitating Paul in relation to how he esteems other leaders and seeks to work with them to accomplish the work of God and maintain the unity of the body of believers. Thus, if they would heed to Paul's appeal the tension in the church would subside and pave the way for a more cordial visit of Paul "'in a spirit of gentleness' instead of 'with a rod.'"[72]

In his conclusion at 1 Corinthians 4:18–21 Paul reiterates his strong warning to those who have continued to be arrogant. Charles A. Wanamaker suggests that the arrogant people whom Paul mentions here refer to "those who pride themselves in their rhetorical sophistication and its concomitant social status and power (1 Cor 4:19) and in turn have apparently demeaned Paul for his lack of eloquence and social status (1 Cor 2:1–5)."[73] Though he is specifically referring to the "arrogant" his final rhetorical questions in 4:21 indicate that Paul is addressing the entire church. These questions are aimed at underscoring his spiritual authority as their "father" who can exercise discipline or demonstrate love and gentleness.

3.5 Summary and Evaluation of Rhetorical Effectiveness

In evaluating the rhetorical effectiveness, the interpreter evaluates whether the rhetoric has effectively addressed the exigencies that it seeks to modify. Is the audience convinced or moved to act toward the desired changes as urged in the rhetoric?

As we have shown, 1 Corinthians 1–4 contains the basic elements of Greco-Roman rhetoric. Seen as a rhetorical unit 1 Corinthians 1–4 has an opening, middle, and closing sections. Paul identifies his relationship with his audience in the opening section, establishes his arguments and admonitions at the middle section, and seals his final emotional appeal in the closing section.

The rhetorical situation has the exigency, audience, and constraints. The situation that prompted Paul to write them is rhetorical because it is an actual situation that compels Paul to respond so it can be modified through a rhetorical discourse. It is a complex situation because it has three interrelated exigencies: the problems of division, boasting, and wisdom. The

---

72. Pickett, *Cross in Corinth*, 84.
73. Wanamaker, "Rhetoric of Power," 115–38.

problem of division is the first exigency. Quarreling among the members of the Corinthian church caused the problem of division. They are quarreling because they are boasting about their missionary workers. The quarreling in the church existed between two groups, the Paul group and the Apollos group. When Paul discusses the problem of boasting in 1 Corinthians 3, he only refers to him and Apollos specifically when he asks especially when he asks in 1 Corinthians 3:4–5, "For when one says, 'I am of Paul,' and another says, 'I am of Apollos,' are you not mere men? What then is Apollos? And What is Paul?" In addition, in 1 Corinthians 4:6, he specifically refers to him and Apollos when he reiterates that they should stop boasting about them because it is causing division in the church. There is no mention in the text that connects the Cephas group or the Christ group to the problems in the church. Those who prefer Apollos are boasting about the rhetorical skills of Apollos while at the same time criticizing Paul. Those who prefer Paul are also boasting about his achievements as the founder of the church in an attempt to assuage the criticisms hurled against Paul. The second exigency is the problem of boasting. They are boasting not just about their missionary workers but also about themselves. They have become puffed up. They examine their own worth and the worth of their missionary workers, Paul and Apollos. They end up boasting about one missionary worker and criticizing the other. Paul explains that there is no reason to boast about him and Apollos because they are all servants of God and together, they are one. Paul appeals in 4:16 with an exhortation to imitate him in the way he sees himself and treats his co-worker. The third exigency is the problem of wisdom. Paul commands the Corinthian believers not to be deceived into thinking they are wise. They think they are wise but their evaluation is based on a false sense of superiority. This false sense of superiority loops back and leads them to boast about their leaders. Here, Paul reiterates that they do not belong to their missionary workers. Instead, their missionary workers belong to all of them and all of them belong to Christ. The audience is the Corinthian believers, but this does not mean the entire church is involved in the exigencies. Paul has the constraints that give him leverage in making sure his message is accepted well and the things he expects them to do are heeded. He is their spiritual father and his relationship with them holds as a bond that allows him to rebuke as well as exhort them.

The species of rhetoric is a combination of deliberative and epideictic rhetoric. Using deliberative rhetoric, Paul exhorts them to act upon the exigencies in order to change and reestablish the unity of the body of Christ. As epideictic rhetoric Paul expresses his thanksgiving for the grace of God at work in their lives. He also denounces their acts calling it similar to the act of people who do not have the Spirit of God. He also affirms his good relationship with Apollos as his co-worker in the Lord. 1 Corinthians 1–4 does not have a stasis because there is no clear accusation against Paul as well as clear defense.

The arrangement of this rhetorical unit also conforms to Greco-Roman rhetoric. Paul uses the *exordium* in 1 Corinthians 1:1–9 to prepare his audience so they are attentive, open, and well-disposed to his message.

At the *propositio* in 1 Corinthians 1:10 Paul appeals to them based on his relationship with them as their apostle and in the name of the Lord Jesus Christ. Drawing on the usual characteristics of deliberative rhetoric, Paul also describes the reasons and the background of the *propositio* at the *narratio* in 1:11–17 as well as how he came to know about the situation at the church. At the *probatio* in 1:18–4:5 Paul confronts the problems of division, wisdom, and boasting head on. Here we see Paul using *inventio* and style in his deliberations to emphasize the futility of the wisdom of the world and points out that the proper way of boasting is in boasting about God who has given them Christ, the wisdom of God, and has caused the growth in the church, not about their missionary workers who are God's servants. He demonstrates well his external proof by appealing to the Scriptures to demonstrate the certainty of God's actions against the wisdom of the world and its futility. He also uses internal proofs (*ethos*, *pathos*, and *logos*). He establishes his integrity and asks questions to highlight that the wisdom of God is superior to the wisdom of the world. At the *peroratio* in 4:6–21 Paul bids his emotional appeal by summing up his arguments, stirring up *indignatio*, and in the *conquestio*, as their father he appeals to their gentle spirit to gain sympathy so they will be moved to agree with one another and resolve the problems of division, boasting and wisdom. Here, we see Paul closing his arguments using παρακαλῶ which he first used in his opening statement at the *exordium*.

So, we ask the question, did Paul persuade the audience to act upon the exigencies to modify them? It is not clear whether the Corinthian believers acted upon the teachings of Paul especially in relation to wisdom. There is no indication elsewhere in 1 Corinthians whether they changed their understanding, ceased from boasting about their missionary workers, or stopped quarreling with each other. In effect, there is no indication that the exigencies have been resolved.

CHAPTER 4

Paul's Wisdom Teaching and the Problems in 1 Corinthians 1–4

In this chapter, I demonstrate how Paul's wisdom teaching provides a key for seeing how the three problems connect. First, I analyze the meaning of Paul's wisdom teaching particularly the meaning of "Christ, the wisdom of God." Second, I establish how these problems fit together and argue that Paul's wisdom concept, particularly his discussion on "Christ, the wisdom of God" is Paul's response not only to the problem of wisdom but also to the problems of division and boasting.

4.1 Paul's Wisdom Teaching

In 1 Corinthians 1:10–17 after briefly pointing out the problem of division where Paul gave his *propositio* that they should agree with one another Paul shifts his discussion to his teaching on wisdom. In 1:17 Paul transitions to his wisdom teaching by emphasizing that God did not send him to baptize but to preach the gospel not relying on wisdom of words so that the cross may not be emptied of its power. As argued in chapter 3, the phrase οὐκ ἐν σοφίᾳ λόγου refers to the manner of speaking that is identified with human ability to make an act of proclamation where success in speaking is based on persuasiveness.

Thiselton suggests three ways to understand ἵνα μὴ κενωθῇ ὁ σταυρὸς τοῦ Χριστοῦ. First, the cross of Christ is nullified of its power when the preaching centers on the skill of the person. Second, the preaching of the gospel based on the cleverness of the speaker may initially persuade the person but may not effect transformation in the life of the person. Third, the preaching of the gospel stands on God's work. It is based on his authority. People must respond to God and not to the eloquence of the speaker. When the preaching is based on human ability and cleverness "the transformative and promissory power of the cross of Christ becomes bypassed and thereby nullified."[1]

In this context the phrase ἵνα μὴ κενωθῇ ὁ σταυρὸς τοῦ Χριστοῦ means that if the message of the cross is preached employing wisdom of words, then the proclamation of the gospel is accomplished not according to the power of God but according to human persuasiveness. The cross is nullified of its power because in the first place the one proclaiming the gospel has not relied on the power of God but on their own persuasiveness. In relation to 1 Corinthians 2:1–5, when the gospel is proclaimed using the wisdom of the world then the faith of those who would respond to the gospel would then be anchored on the wisdom of the world and not on the power of God. Thus, Paul did not resort to a method popular in his time because he understands that God wants him to do God's work according to God's method. The message of the cross is not intended to move people to respond to it based on the eloquence of the speaker but to point people to respond in faith to Christ himself.

Raymond Collins suggests that the reason why the proclamation of the cross is foolishness to the perishing because in the ancient time crucifixion was sentenced to those who were considered political enemies and rebels. It usually applies only to the "lower classes of society, particularly slaves and unruly criminals."[2] These people were flogged and hanged naked until death. Many did not get decent burials afterward.[3] They were punished publicly to warn the crowd against violating and disrespecting the power and the authority of the Roman government. It was set to impose the sovereignty of the Roman government over every person.[4] In a culture where public honor was of high value the cross was absurd. They could not comprehend how a powerful God would succumb to a shameful redemptive plan.[5] Paul's message lacks in persuasiveness based on the standards of the wisdom of the

---

1. Thiselton, *First Corinthians*, 145–46.
2. Collins, *First Corinthians*, 91.
3. Collins, *First Corinthians*, 92.
4. Hays, "Wisdom According to Paul," 115.
5. Ciampa and Rosner, *First Letter*, 91. Cf. Green, "Folly of the Cross," 59–69.

world. Thus, to the current audience of Paul the proclamation of the cross is merely one of the wisdom teachings that they could not make sense of so they consider it foolishness.

4.1.1 Wisdom of the World and Wisdom of God

In terms of content, Paul's wisdom teaching revolves around the discussion on how humans can know or cannot know God. In terms of function, Paul's wisdom teaching addresses the Corinthian believer's understanding of wisdom in relation to salvation as well as their false sense of superiority and understanding of what it means to be wise in relation to the problems of the church.

In 1 Corinthians 1:19–23 Paul refers to how God has made the wisdom of the world foolish. He emphasized that God has declared its destruction and its inability to know God. That is, God cannot be known unless he reveals himself to humanity.

What does Paul mean by the phrase τὴν σοφίαν τοῦ κόσμου? Collins presents some of the views of the scholars. First, it is possible Paul could be talking here about "Jewish wisdom tradition (Hans Conzelmann, Jacques Dupont, Andre Feuillet, Hans Windisch)."[6] Second, wisdom of the world may refer to "wisdom tradition found in Hellenistic Judaism and reflected in the writings of Paul's contemporary, Philo of Alexandria (Richard Horsley, Birger A. Pearson, James A. Davis)."[7] Third, this phrase could refer to "Jewish wisdom tradition combined with apocalyptic elements that had had an impact on the Corinthians (Scroggs) while others think that a confluence of apocalyptic and philosophical elements was the source of the wisdom valued by the Corinthians (Alexandra R. Brown)."[8] Fourth, the phrase could also point to "Gnosticism, perhaps in some primitive form of Gnosticism (Wilhelm Lutgert, Rudolf Bultmann, Walter Schmithals, Ulrich Wilckens, Bruce W. Winter)."[9] Collins suggests that while these views present insights about the meaning of the phrase τὴν σοφίαν τοῦ κόσμου it is best to see this in view of Paul's statement in 1 Corinthians 1:17. That is, Paul is referring to how people

---

6. Collins, *First Corinthians*, 96.
7. Collins, *First Corinthians*, 96.
8. Collins, *First Corinthians*, 97
9. Collins, *First Corinthians*, 97.

in his time rely on human persuasiveness to effectively convey the message and move people to respond to it.[10]

John Polhill suggests that Paul's intention in this section is to address the misconception of the "locus of salvation." That is, Paul needs to confront the belief regarding "the substitution of human wisdom, philosophy, and rhetoric for the divine plan of salvation in Christ."[11] It is clear that Paul is discussing here the message of the cross and the Christ crucified from 1 Corinthians 1:17 to 1:24. Throughout this section, Paul's discussion focuses on important themes such as that the wisdom of the world has been made foolish by God because it cannot know God and Christ crucified is the wisdom and power of God. In this regard, it is difficult to establish that Paul's wisdom teaching is a polemic against the wrong concept of the locus of salvation. It is not an issue here. The wisdom of the world's failure to know God, the message of the cross, and the crucified Christ does not refer to their quest for salvation. In fact, they do not even make it their quest to begin with. It is because their failure to know the wisdom of God refers to their understanding that the message of the cross is foolishness. Since it is foolishness, they would not accept or embrace it. Rather they reject it. Does it mean they are seeking salvation by pursuing rhetoric? It is not clear either. From a sociohistorical perspective, there is no indication too that people were pursuing rhetoric for soteriological purposes.

In 1 Corinthians 1:21 the phrase ἐν τῇ σοφίᾳ τοῦ θεοῦ has drawn various views from many authors. Thiselton summarizes them. First, the phrase may refer to how wisdom is revealed according to the law and the prophets (Clement and Chrysostom). Second, it may refer to the transformational effect of wisdom in reversing the value system of the world (Origen). Third, it may refer to how God acts in revealing himself. Humans do not have the capability to know God or discern his way unless God reveals himself. Human wisdom is not capable of saving the person apart from the wisdom of God (Conzelmann, Barth, Barrett, Calvin, and Davis).[12] Fourth, it may refer to the wisdom of God "as a prophetic critique of instrumental reason."[13]

---

10. Collins, *First Corinthians*, 97.
11. Polhill, "Wisdom of God," 329.
12. Thiselton, *First Corinthians*, 167–68.
13. Thiselton, *First Corinthians*, 169.

Human wisdom claims the ability to master life and its problems but in the wisdom of God, the power to master life and its problems relies on God (Beaudean). Fifth, it may refer to the wisdom of God "as grace freely given" (Litfin, Welborn and Jüngel).[14] Similar to option three, wisdom is seen as God's work in the life of the individual. It takes the focus away from man's eloquence and knowledge and puts it on God's work done on the cross through Christ.[15]

The different views presented by Thiselton contain concepts related to salvation and the proclamation of the cross. It provides links between wisdom and salvation. Among these views, the third view appears to be more consistent with what Paul wants to communicate to the Corinthians believers. The context shows that Paul's emphasis is on how God used divine wisdom as a means to make the wisdom of the world foolish. In 1:20 Paul establishes the limitations of the wisdom of the world in knowing God when he asks, "Where is the wise man? Where is the scribe? Where is the debater of this age?" These questions must be understood in light of 1:21 where God has declared the way of the wisdom of the world (human wisdom) a failure. It is God's design that without the wisdom of God it is impossible for humans to know God. Thus, the phrase ἐν τῇ σοφίᾳ τοῦ θεοῦ demonstrates the act of God in excluding the wisdom of the world in knowing him. God only reveals himself to those who believe. Barrett explains that God's wisdom has accomplished what the wisdom of the world failed to accomplish. God made the wisdom of the world foolish "by doing this in a way by which the wise men of the world dismissed as foolish."[16]

Also, the phrase ἐν τῇ σοφίᾳ τοῦ θεοῦ points ahead to Paul's reference to Christ in 1:24, where Christ is the "power of God and wisdom of God." In this sense Paul affirms that God can only be known through Christ, the "power of God and wisdom of God." Everyone stands equally helpless in the sight of God apart from Christ. David Garland aptly says, "In the cross, God puts both Jew and Greek, wise and foolish, trained and untrained, on the same level, canceling out all human enlightenment on the subject of salvation or

---

14. Thiselton, *First Corinthians*, 169.
15. Thiselton, *First Corinthians*, 169.
16. Barrett, *Commentary on the First Epistle*, 53.

redemption."[17] Thus, only those who believe in the message of the cross, which the wisdom of world considers foolishness, are saved. Here, Paul builds on his earlier statement where he compared how those who are perishing and being saved consider the proclamation of the cross.

In 1 Corinthians 1:22–23, Paul reiterates how wisdom of the world has continually failed to know God. The Jews, even though some of them have witnessed the crucifixion as well as the resurrection, are still asking for sign because the proclamation of the cross is a stumbling block to them. Gentiles search for wisdom. It has been preached to them yet they could not understand it because it is foolishness to them. Witherington explains that it is grossly offensive for the Jews to think of a crucified messiah because they have been looking and waiting for the messiah who will defeat his enemies, "not be executed by them."[18] Likewise, the cross is considered foolishness for the Gentiles because it does not make sense that a powerful God or messiah could easily fall into the hands of his captors and suffer "the ultimate penalty from Rome."[19] Donald E. Green adds that Paul's message of the crucified Christ appears absurd and ridiculous both to the Jews and Gentiles. He writes, "Jews had to abandon their notions of a curse being upon the crucified, the Gentiles had to abandon their associations of weakness and contempt before they could believe in Christ. It was simply preposterous to suggest that this crucifixion was the focal point of the redemption of mankind."[20] Paul's metaphor of the Jews and Gentiles having a hard time making sense of the message of the cross essentially illustrates the incapability of the wisdom of the world to comprehend God. It essentially elaborates how the message of the cross came to be perceived as foolishness by those who are perishing.

The phrase Χριστον θεοῦ δύναμιν in 1 Corinthians 1:24 may be referred to two possible things: the resurrection of Christ, which displays the power of God, or Christ being the power of God unto salvation. Based on the context, the latter is more probable. Paul was not merely pointing them to the cross as the wisdom of God but "on the actual effective work of the cross in the

---

17. Garland, *1 Corinthians*, 67.
18. Witherington, *Conflict and Community*, 109.
19. Witherington, *Conflict and Community*, 109.
20. Green, "Folly of the Cross," 67.

world."²¹ Christ became the wisdom of God because Christ crucified is the power of God for the salvation of those who have been called.

Here in 1 Corinthians 1:24 recalling Paul's statement that proclaiming the cross is the power of God for those being saved (1 Cor 1:18), the phrase "power of God" emphasizes that to those being saved (1 Cor 1:18), that is, those who believe (1 Cor 1:21), and are called, the crucified Christ is the means by which they can know God. In this manner, the wisdom that the world considers foolish is wiser and the wisdom that the world considers weak is stronger. In addition, the term "Christ, the wisdom of God" defines who Christ is to those who believe and it establishes the fact that as far as wisdom is concerned everything that humans seek about wisdom is in Christ because he is the wisdom of God. This seals the argument that any pursuit of wisdom apart from Christ is futile.

In 1 Corinthians 1:26 Paul says that most members of the church were not wise, mighty, and noble in the eyes of the world when they came to know Christ. As discussed in chapter 2, I postulated that the words "wise, powerful, and noble" refers to the wealthy patrons of the different house churches that were influenced by rhetoric. Paul wants them to understand that in view of 1 Corinthians 1:21, in as much as the wise, scribe, and debater of this age whom Paul says could not know God apart from Christ, none of the members of the Corinthian church, as well even the ones who are wise, mighty, and noble, have come to know God through the wisdom of the world but through Christ alone.

In 1 Corinthians 1:27–29, the threefold use of the phrase ἐξελέξατο ὁ θεός emphasizes the divine act of God in choosing the foolish things of the world to shame the wise, the strong, and the noble to establish the fact that God's sovereign choice is not based on human achievements or credentials but on the wisdom of God. On an important note, the phrase "foolish things of the world" does not necessarily refer to the Corinthian believers. There is nothing in the text that suggests this notion.²² The reading does not make sense if it were to be taken this way because as indicated above many of the members of the church from different social levels are involved in the quarreling as a result of their propensity to the wisdom of the world. Paul's use of the phrase

---

21. Fee, *First Epistle*, 77. Cf. Ellis, *Prophecy and Hermeneutic*, 73.
22. Cf. O'Day, "Jeremiah," 259–67.

"foolish things of the world" shows his rhetorical method of contrasting the nature of wisdom of the world and wisdom of God to heighten the fact that the wisdom of God stands superior over the wisdom of the world. Thus, as expressed in the context Paul's purpose in emphasizing God's divine prerogative is not just in the sense of choosing people for salvation but also in nullifying any "possibility of human self-glorification."[23] Pickett affirms this statement when he writes, "By disclosing the divine wisdom and power in the cross of Christ and choosing the weak and foolish of the world, God has undermined all grounds of human boasting, especially the secular values which were the basis of the Corinthians' arrogance."[24]

The word καταισχύνη in 1 Cor 1:27 must not be understood in light of the social concept of shame. Honor is very important to the Corinthian people but the shaming of God here does not refer specifically to this. Shaming here carries the "sense of being condemned by God in judgment" when it is understood in view of Paul's use of the word καταργήσῃ.[25] Here, the progression of Paul's argument in demonstrating not only the sovereign work of God in calling them in Christ but also in refuting any reason to boast based on human achievements is seen in Paul's use of the word καταισχύνη in 1:27 and καταργήσῃ in 1:28. Paul reiterates God's final verdict by using καταργήσῃ in the last phrase in place of καταισχύνη, which he uses in the first two phrases. Thus, shaming the wise, powerful, and noble means that they have nothing to trust or boast upon in the presence of God.[26] In this divine act of choosing the nobodies over the somebodies, God nullified everything that the wisdom of the world could boast of in order to demonstrate that the wisdom of the world is rubbish.

Paul's emphasis is not only on the sovereignty of God to choose people but also on God's definitive work of disarming the value system of the world and asserting his sovereignty in prescribing the divine system by which every human must abide. Veronica Koperski writes,

> In 1 Cor he is trying to tell the Corinthians this is something they should have known from *their own* experience . . . Paul

---

23. Conzelmann, *1 Corinthians*, 50–51.
24. Pickett, *Cross in Corinth*, 74.
25. Ciampa and Rosner, *First Letter*, 107.
26. Inkelaar, *Conflict over Wisdom*, 207–8.

asserts that those who demand signs, as well as those who take pride in seeking after an eloquent pseudo-wisdom (1 Cor 1:22), have misunderstood the meaning of *being chosen*; they should remember their own experience: God chose the foolish things of this world; God chose the weak; God chose what is low and despised, even the things that are not (1 Cor 1:27–28).[27]

To this effect, none of them could boast. It is God's divine design that no one would have any basis to boast about knowing God. God has precluded any manner by which knowing God can be obtained apart from Christ.[28]

In 1 Corinthians 1:30 Paul solidifies the argument that everything is God's work by recalling his earlier statement about Christ is the wisdom of God. Thiselton takes the phrase "Christ Jesus, who became to us wisdom from God" to mean that Christ is the source of wisdom from God, and connects it with 1:31. He explains, "Wisdom is redefined and explicated as receiving the gifts of righteousness, sanctification, and redemption freely bestowed through Christ and derivative from him . . . Hence to glory in their new-found status as righteous, holy, and redeemed is to glory in the Lord, and in no other person, no other thing."[29] What Thiselton says however fails to notice the flow and context of Paul's arguments. If we take this to mean that Christ is the source of wisdom from God, then Paul seems to deviate from his discussion and introduces a new concept about Christ. That is, from being the wisdom of God to being the source of wisdom for us from God. It is difficult to follow Paul's arguments here if this is the case.

Following Paul's flow of thought the phrase ἐν Χριστῷ Ἰησοῦ, ὃς ἐγενήθη σοφία ἡμῖν ἀπὸ θεοῦ recalls Paul's earlier statement in 1 Corinthians 1:24 where he highlighted the role of Christ in the salvation for those who believe. Here, the phrase ἐν Χριστῷ is taken as Christ is the means of righteousness, sanctification, and redemption. Fee claims

> These are not three different steps in the saving process; they are rather three different metaphors for the same event (our salvation that was effected in Christ) . . . The fact that he uses nouns

---

27. Koperski, "Knowledge of Christ," 383–84.
28. Clarke, *Secular and Christian Leadership*, 95–97.
29. Thiselton, *First Corinthians*, 192.

to describe this event, rather than verbs, is dictated by the fact that they stand in apposition to the noun "wisdom."[30]

Fee did not elaborate though why he calls them metaphors. However, the words, righteousness, sanctification, and redemption, could not be metaphors because these are what believers receive from God through Christ.

Adam G. White observes that the terms righteousness, sanctification, and redemption distinctly distinguishes Christ, the wisdom of God, from the wisdom of the world. In the wisdom of the world human needs to seek and pursue wisdom but in God he has made Christ the wisdom for us. As indicated in the passive sense, Christ has become wisdom for us from God and God gives righteousness, sanctification, and redemption freely through Christ the wisdom of God.[31]

Does this mean that if believers at Corinth were in Christ they would become wise or increase in their understanding of God? The context shows that the wisdom of God is not about pursuing wisdom for personal or human gains through human means. Rather it is the pursuit of God and, as will be revealed in 1 Corinthians 2, a divine work that is made possible through the work of the Spirit of God. As Hays says, "There is no such thing as 'wisdom' apart from covenant relationship with God ('righteousness') that leads to holy living ('sanctification') made possible by God's act of delivering us from slavery ('redemption') through the cross."[32] In view of the situation in the Corinthian church, this clarifies the fact that the pursuit of wisdom is not focused on acquiring knowledge and skills as is often the case in the world. Rather, it is the pursuit of God through Christ, who is the wisdom of God, through whom the believers receive righteousness, sanctification, and redemption. The pursuit of wisdom is not initiated by humans (where they strive to be eloquent in rhetoric and gain more knowledge of the wisdom of the world) but initiated by God. As one person becomes a recipient of righteousness, sanctification, and redemption through the wisdom of God, they initiate a relationship with other people that expresses the very nature of the wisdom of God. In this context, one important issue raised by Paul is how the pursuit of the wisdom of God has brought Jews and Greeks together

---

30. Fee, *First Epistle*, 86.
31. White, *Where is the Wise Man?*, 79–81.
32. Hays, "Wisdom According to Paul," 117.

in Christ. They were united because they believed in the message of the cross. Essentially, Paul is saying in the wisdom of God there is no division irrespective of race, ethnicity, and skills in human persuasiveness (eloquence in rhetoric). Every believer belongs to Christ and there is no reason to boast, quarrel, or be divided.

What is the significance of the phrase "Christ Jesus, who became to us wisdom from God, and righteousness and sanctification, and redemption" to the Corinthian believers in view of their situation? It clarifies that everything they have been trying to become by pursuing the wisdom of the world is already in Christ and received through Christ. Rhetorically, Paul emphasizes that righteousness, sanctification, and redemption are only received through Christ from God. Thus, no one can boast. If one must boast, let him boast in the Lord for what God has done and given him through Christ. James Davis notes that Paul's exhortation about not boasting must be understood in light of his reference to Christ, the wisdom of God in 1 Corinthians 1:30 where those "who 'boast in the Lord' boast in their understanding of God's act in Christ in which a new wisdom has come into being, providing life, righteousness, holiness, and redemption."[33]

Beginning with 1 Corinthians 1:26, Paul elaborates the sovereign work of God that though they were not wise, mighty, and noble yet God chose them and called them in Christ who became God's wisdom for humanity. Through Christ, they have become people of the wisdom of God and they were given righteousness, sanctification, and redemption. In view of this, Paul redefines how the Corinthian Christians must see themselves and how they treat one another and their missionary workers. That is, they must cease from boasting about themselves and their missionary workers because they are no longer people of the wisdom of the world but of the wisdom of God.[34] In this manner, Paul did not only demolish their reason to boast about themselves or their missionary workers but also provide them an explicit reason to boast only in the Lord. We can almost hear Paul saying, "How can you then boast in anything else but in the Lord?"[35]

---

33. Davis, *Wisdom and Spirit*, 78.
34. Collins, *First Corinthians*, 99.
35. Inkelaar, *Conflict over Wisdom*, 206.

4.1.2 The Spirit of God and the Wisdom of God

Here in 1 Corinthians 2:1–5 Paul wants his readers to understand the reason why he did not proclaim the gospel according to human persuasion. Paul explains that proclaiming the gospel through the power of God is God's divine way of bringing people to a life of faith that rests on the wisdom of God. In addition, Paul explains that, when he preached the gospel, he did not rely on human persuasiveness but on the power of God because his sole preoccupation was not about himself or anything else but on his gospel, the crucified Christ. Conzelmann notes this decision is "not arbitrary" but based on "his understanding of the message, on the ground of the cross."[36] This recalls 1 Corinthians 1:17 where Paul clearly stated that God sent him to preach the gospel without relying on human persuasiveness because the gospel is inherently the power of God.

According to Thiselton, Paul is not just making a statement here about the nature of his proclamation but also claiming that they themselves can testify how he preached the gospel.[37] The word ὑπεροχὴν in this context may refer not only to the superiority of proclamation but also to the superiority of the one proclaiming. It could mean that Paul did not come with superiority of style especially with reference to his claim that came in weakness, fear, and much trembling.[38] It highlights Paul's intention to distinguish himself and his preaching from the common practice of their time where rhetors rely on the use of superiority of speech to persuade or entertain the hearers. That is, Paul did not rely on his ability to persuade them but on the power of God. The proclamation of the cross possesses a superior persuasiveness to convict people. As such there is no need for human intervention for it to be effective. Koperski explains that when Paul mentions he did not preach the gospel with the "superiority of speech" he was "perhaps implying that what he proclaims does not need to be presented with rhetorical artifice; its sublimity, or excellence, is inherent."[39] William Orr and James Arthur Walther assert Paul's purpose is to show the Corinthian believers that his preaching did not rely on his ability to speak or his style to make himself convincing to the crowd for

---

36. Conzelmann, *1 Corinthians*, 54.
37. Thiselton, *First Corinthians*, 208.
38. White, *Where Is the Wise Man?*, 102.
39. Koperski, "Knowledge of Christ," 377–96.

it was intended to point them to Christ, not to himself. It was intended not to entertain but to convict them to turn to God.[40] Paul did not consider his method as a disadvantage because the power of God was revealed through it.[41] As a summary, Ciampa and Rosner write,

> With 2:5 the series of contrasts that Paul introduced in 1:17 is thus complete: Paul's gospel comes: (1) not with (human) wisdom, but with (God's) foolishness, (2) not with (the world's) power, but with (Paul's and God's) weakness, (3) not to the things that are, but to the things that are not, and (4) not with a demonstration of rhetorical skill, but with a demonstration of the Spirit's power.[42]

What does Paul mean by "mature" in 1 Corinthians 2:6? H. A. W. Meyer says that mature refers to "those who have penetrated beyond the position of beginners in Christ saving knowledge to the higher sphere of thorough and comprehensive insight."[43] Thus, this "wisdom" is suitable for the "mature," not for the beginners in Christ.[44] Based on the context τελείοις are the ones who received the Spirit (1 Cor 2:12) and therefore, spiritual people (1 Cor 2:15). Hence, the τελείοις can understand the wisdom of God because the Spirit of God reveals the wisdom of God to them.

The reference to the "rulers of the age" in 1 Corinthians 2:8 invites a deeper look at the implication of the phrase. Considering Paul's rhetorical method, the reference to the "rulers of this age" focuses on how Paul paints the stark contrast between the wisdom of God and the wisdom of the world. In light of the context, this phrase accentuates two important points. First, it heightens the futility of the wisdom of the world. If the rulers of this age understood the wisdom of God, they would not have crucified the Lord of glory. By pointing out their inability to understand the wisdom of God Paul intensifies the fact that God's wisdom is superior to the wisdom of the world because even the

---

40. Orr and Walther, *1 Corinthians*, 163.
41. Garland, *1 Corinthians*, 85.
42. Ciampa and Rosner, *First Letter*, 119. Cf. Horsley, "Wisdom of Word," 224–39.
43. Meyer, *Critical and Exegetical Hand-book*, 47
44. Meyer, *Critical and Exegetical Hand-book*, 47. Cf. Pearson, *Pneumatikos-Psychikos Terminology*, 27–31.

rulers of this age cannot understand it.⁴⁵ Second, it re-echoes Paul's earlier declaration in 1 Corinthians 1:23–24 about the crucified Christ who is the wisdom of God: "But we preached Christ crucified, a stumbling block to the Jews and foolishness to the Gentiles, but to those who are the called, both Jews and Greeks, Christ the power of God and the wisdom of God." Daniel J. Ebert IV aptly summarizes it when he writes, "Paul's wisdom teaching is . . . about the entire drama of salvation as it is played out in Christ. Wisdom is in the crucifixion of Christ, with all of its implication for the church and the world, and with the proclamation of that message. This is the wisdom of God."⁴⁶

The term wisdom, as Meyer suggests, refers to wisdom in contrast to the rhetoric of the wisdom of world. Referring to 1 Corinthians 2:13 Meyer refers to wisdom as a "spiritual discourse (ver. 13) framed under the influence of the holy πνεῦμα . . . and its matter was the future relations of the Messianic kingdom."⁴⁷ Meyer (also Barrett) considers this message exclusively intended for the mature only because infants in Christ are not yet ready to receive it.⁴⁸ Ciampa and Rosner agree with Meyer by saying "the message of wisdom is the full scope of God's teaching on salvation and the Christian life, which only 'the mature' digest and appropriate."⁴⁹ Scroggs suggests that this is Paul's esoteric message intended only for the τελείοι due to the fact that there are no references outside of 1 Corinthians where Paul has taught his wisdom teaching to another group of audience. There are no references of similar teaching by Paul of this sort can be found elsewhere except here in 1 Corinthians 2:6–16. It is probable that he has a separate teaching for the entire church and for the selected τελείοι whom Paul considers as "ethically and disciplined Christian, [and] obedient to the kerygma."⁵⁰ This is probably the reason Paul is not able to address the Corinthian believers in wisdom in 1 Corinthians 2:14–3:4 because they lack the comprehension only the mature ones possess. However, Collins argues Paul has consistently referred to

---

45. Cf. Scroggs, "Paul," 41–44.

46. Ebert, *Wisdom Christology*, 66. Cf. Given, *Paul's True Rhetoric*, 100; Grindheim, "Wisdom for the Perfect," 689–709.

47. Meyer, *Critical and Exegetical Handbook*, 47.

48. Meyer, *Critical and Exegetical Handbook*, 47; Barrett, *Commentary on the First Epistle*, 69.

49. Ciampa and Rosner, *First Letter*, 123.

50. Scroggs, "Paul," 37–38.

a single audience and message. "He does not espouse a two-tier view of the Christian community with an eschatological message being addressed to the perfect and the basic teachings essential for Christian life being addressed to others."[51] According to Orr and Walther, to imply Paul is alluding to two kinds of believers in the church also suggests two kinds of wisdom message, the proclamation of the cross for everyone and new deeper wisdom for the mature. This concept is foreign to Paul's language in this section. Paul's discussion on wisdom centers on Christ crucified beginning with 1 Corinthians 1. For Paul, the wisdom of God is "contained in the message of the cross." Hence, the τελείοις are the ones who have "embraced the message of the cross."[52] Thus, Paul is not talking about two kinds of wisdom. Rather Paul is talking about one wisdom only but perceived by the τελείοις in 2:6 and the νηπίοις in 3:1 differently. William Baird explains,

> In I Corinthians 2:6 ff. Paul divides those who are being saved into the mature and the immature Christians. Thus, when he seems to speak of a special sort of wisdom in verse 6, in truth, he is referring to the proclamation of the crucified Christ. To the spiritually immature this seems like a simple message – to these babes in Christ it is mere "milk." To the mature it is "solid food" indeed – it is the hidden wisdom of God foreordained before the ages and revealed through the Spirit to those who have the mind of Christ. The distinction is not in the wisdom, but in its recipients.[53]

Here in 1 Corinthians 2:6–16 Paul continues to emphasize that this wisdom of God is the kind of wisdom that cannot be discerned based on human understanding unless God reveals it. Paul focuses on the role of the Spirit of God in the revelation of wisdom and explains why humans cannot understand the wisdom of God. Thus, it is hidden. Barrett explains, "It is *hidden* in the sense that it has only been disclosed at the turning of the ages, in the recent

---

51. Collins, *First Corinthians*, 128.
52. Orr and Walther, *1 Corinthians*, 163–64.
53. Baird, "Among the Mature," 425–32. Cf. Grindheim, "Wisdom for the Perfect," 689–709; Williams, *Paul's Metaphors*, 59–60.

historical event of Christ crucified; hidden also in that it has nothing to do with *persuasive words of wisdom* (ii. 4)."[54]

Paul continually exposes with emphasis the limitation of the wisdom of the world in knowing the wisdom of God. This is the reason why in 2:8 the rulers of the age crucified Christ. They did not understand that Christ crucified, the power of God and wisdom of God, is God's agent for the salvation of humanity. This is where Paul continues to disarm the wisdom of the world. The wisdom of the world cannot understand the wisdom of God because they do not have the revelation of the Spirit. Paul explains that wisdom of God is beyond the reach of the wisdom of the world and can only be known through the Spirit. Thus, the spiritual person is the one who understands the wisdom of God because the Spirit of God reveals it to him.

Paul's logic is clear: just as no one knows the thoughts of one person unless he reveals it to another person, so only God knows the thoughts of God unless God reveals it through the Holy Spirit. Thiselton adds, "We cannot expect that God's own thought's, God's own purposes, God's own qualities, or God's own self could be open to scrutiny unless his spirit makes them accessible by an act of unveiling them."[55]

4.1.3 The Boasting of People and the Wisdom of God

Building on his discourse in 1 Corinthians 2:6–16, Paul now applies the implications of the Spirit of God to the lives of the Corinthian believers in 1 Corinthians 3:1–5. He opens this section with a candid rebuke of their conduct in the church. He sounds disappointed because of the ignominious fact that he could not call them "spiritual men" but "men of flesh, as to infants in Christ."[56] The context shows that Paul's use of the word νηπίοις must be viewed in light of the word τελείοις in 2:6 and πνευματικοῖς in 2:15. In fact, in 3:1 Paul clarifies the contrast between the πνευματικοῖς and the σαρκίνοις.

That the Corinthian believers are infants in Christ needs further clarification. As explained in the rhetorical analysis earlier, Paul's approach in calling them νηπίοις is meant to rebuke them for their immaturity. It is not meant to strip or deny them of their status as believers in Christ and consider them

---

54. Barrett, *Commentary on the First Epistle*, 71.
55. Thiselton, *First Corinthians*, 259.
56. Cf. Barclay, *Pauline Churches*, 213–14.

pagans. In a sense, Paul alludes to the fact that they have received the gospel and understood the message of the cross yet they have not realized the implications of their conduct to the gospel they received. As people who have received the gospel then, they are expected to demonstrate spiritual, moral, and intellectual transformation through the work of the Holy Spirit. Yet their conduct in the church reflects a life which deeds are incompatible with the deeds of the spiritual men.

Thus, Paul is not talking about their lack of spiritual progress but their failure to live mature spiritual lives. J. Francis elaborates that Paul is addressing their "being childish, a condition contrary to being spiritual . . . a state of immaturity incompatible with that of spiritual understanding."[57] Their jealousy, strife, and boastings illustrate that they are not spiritual as they claim to be but they are people who lack the guidance of the Spirit.[58]

In chapter 2, I presented the social background of 1 Corinthians 1–4 particularly the sophistic movement during their time. I argued that the divisive conduct of the Corinthian believers is similar to the divisive conduct of those who were involved in the sophistic activities. The behavior of the Corinthian believers that Paul compares to merely human behavior seems to reflect the loyalty of first-century disciples of the sophists. In as much as these disciples disparaged other teachers and held to the supremacy of their admired teachers the Corinthian believers also criticize one another and other missionary workers, and particularly Paul. In view of the behavior of the Corinthian believers towards one another and towards other missionary workers in the church, Winter suggests some probable reasons why they conduct themselves in this manner. First, the Corinthian believers have misunderstood how the missionary workers relate to each other. They are not competing against one another but working together to fulfill God's work at Corinth. Also, none of them belong exclusively to one group but all belong to the body of Christ, that is, the believers at Corinth which belongs to Christ.

Second, they have misunderstood the status of the missionary workers. None is above another based on human credentials that probably center on rhetorical abilities. None is greater for all are servants of Christ. So, none of

---

57. Francis, "'Babes in Christ,'" 41–60.

58. Fitzmyer, *First Corinthians*, 170; Litfin, *St. Paul's Theology*, 181–82; cf. Dahl, "Paul and the Church," 320.

the Corinthian believers should boast about one missionary worker above the others because the workers belong to the same category. In fact, when Paul referred to himself and other missionary workers he did not say, "Who is Apollos or who is Paul?" Instead Paul asks, "What, then, is Apollos? And what is Paul?" Paul's questions point them to an important reality that it is not about their status but about their roles in the lives of the believers. They are called by the Lord to perform different roles essential to the growth of believers. Paul captures the whole thought by directing their attention to the most important element in this process: God causes the growth. So, if they should boast, they should boast in the Lord.

In addition to their role as servants of Christ they are also stewards of the mysteries of God. Both roles, servant and steward, center on their calling to minister to the Corinthian believers. This strengthens the idea that the focus of ministry is not themselves as the missionary workers but the Corinthian believers whom God has entrusted to the missionary workers. As Paul declares, they are God's workers and the believers are God's field, God's building.

Third, they have misunderstood Paul's method of proclaiming the gospel and his purpose of proclaiming the gospel in that manner. They have misconstrued his method as a demonstration of weakness. They thought Paul was inferior when compared to other missionary workers and thus they inferred he probably lacked the wisdom and spirituality. Paul emphasized that his purpose was to point the Corinthian believers to the crucified Christ not by means of human persuasiveness but by the demonstration of the power of God.

Fourth, they have misunderstood their relationship to their missionary workers. In the entire discourse, Paul did not call any of them his disciple. This is probably intentional to distinguish between himself and the sophists as well as between the Corinthian believers and the disciples of the sophists. Paul calls them his brothers and his children to make a point that their relationship with one another is anchored on the crucified Christ, the wisdom of God. This further accentuates the fact that all missionary workers are one in Christ as well as all Corinthian believers. Thus, no one should boast about one leader against another but only boast in the Lord.[59]

---

59. Winter, *After Paul Left*, 40–43. Cf. Sanders, "Imitating Paul," 354–55.

In 1 Corinthians 3:18–21, Paul recaps his discussion on wisdom in relation to boasting, which leads to division. Concluding his discussion on wisdom, Paul points out the absurdity of pursuing the wisdom of the world by cautioning the Corinthian believers about being deceived in their thinking.

At this point, Paul shifts from addressing the Corinthian believers as a whole to addressing them as individuals. As asserted earlier in chapter 2, Paul is writing to the whole church and not on any specific group. Particularly in 1 Corinthians 3, whenever Paul addresses the Corinthians believers he addresses them as a whole as indicated by the plural form of εἰμί (1 Cor 3:3–4, 9, 16). However, in 3:18 and 3:21, Paul's commands about not being deceived and ceasing to boast about men are in the singular form. Paul's shift from the plural address to the singular address signals that he is not only addressing them as a group but also addressing some individuals. In this case, Paul is addressing the ones who are boasting and involved in the quarreling in the church. More particularly, he is also addressing the individual patrons whom Paul calls the wise, powerful, and the noble in 1:26 who are leading the groups in boasting about him or Apollos as well as those who criticize him. These household patron leaders are believed to be the ones leading the quarrels among house churches because of their propensity to be drawn to the wisdom of the world. Thus, Paul warns them not to be deceived into thinking that they are already wise because of their proficiency in rhetoric.

Being "deceived" in this context refers to believing in the false idea that possessing the wisdom of the world makes a person truly wise.[60] Only when one chooses to be a fool, that is, to believe in the paradoxical nature of the wisdom of God, Christ crucified, a stumbling block to the Jews and foolishness to the Greeks, that they can be truly wise. Hans-Christoph Askani adds, "it is only when you are a fool that you are not a fool *before* God; And if you are not a fool, you are being foolish (before God)."[61] In 3:18–21 Paul clarifies that the path toward becoming wise is by embracing what is considered foolishness. That is, if one wants to become truly wise they must embrace the message of the cross and pursue the wisdom of God, which the wisdom of the world considers foolishness. Barclay writes, "To align oneself with the message of Christ crucified is not just to sidestep the wisdom framework of

---

60. Cf. BDAG, s.v. "ἐξαπατάω."
61. Askani, "Paradox of Faith," 341–58.

the world, but to disturb its claims and to confront its hegemony: 'if anyone thinks he is wise in this age, *let him become a fool*, in order that he may be wise' (3:18)."[62]

In this context Paul alludes to the fact that the pursuit of the wisdom of the world leads to boasting among people, which is what was happening in the church. Paul's command to stop boasting about their leaders refers back to the different slogans of the people as mentioned in 1 Corinthians 1:12 that emphasizes that these things are not manifestations of the wisdom of God because it promotes division. Rather, in Christ who is the wisdom of God there is no boasting that results in division because everything belongs to God (3:21–22).

Paul clarifies that boasting about people is a misunderstanding of who they are in Christ. Consequently, there is no reason to boast and quarrel about their missionary workers because they all belong to them in the one body of Christ. As people who belong to Christ, all things belong to them as well. Thus, as Fee says, "They may not say 'I belong to Paul, or Apollos, or Cephas,' not only because that is to boast in mere men, but because that is the precise opposite of reality in Christ."[63]

4.1.4 Summary of Paul's Wisdom Teaching

Paul presents his wisdom teaching in view of how God reveals himself so that people may know him. Notwithstanding its eloquence and knowledge, the wisdom of the world failed to know God. God's superior wisdom precludes the wisdom of the world as a way of knowing him and depends on God's self-revelation through the wisdom of God, that is, Christ crucified. It is God's design that the wise man, the scribe, and the debater of this age, even if they claim to possess a superior wisdom, they cannot know God unless God chooses to reveal himself to them. God's design that he can be known only when he chooses to reveal himself to the people highlights not only God's sovereign choice to determine who can know him but also how he can be known. There is nothing the wisdom of the world can do to know God unless God wills it. In this sense, no members of the Corinthian church even those

---

62. Barclay, "Crucifixion as Wisdom," 1–20.
63. Fee, *First Epistle*, 153.

who are wise, mighty, and noble have come to know God by means of the wisdom of the world but because of the wisdom of God alone.

Paul asserts that Christ is the "power of God and wisdom of God." Christ, being the power of God, is the means by which people can know God. This is anchored on Paul's statement in 1:18 that the proclamation of the cross is the power of God to those who are being saved. To the Jews the preaching of the crucified Christ is a stumbling block and to the Gentiles it is foolishness but to those who are being saved (1:18), to those who believe (1:21), and to those who are called the crucified Christ is the power and wisdom of God through whom they can know God. Also, Christ, being the wisdom of God, is the embodiment of the wisdom of God and those who believe and those who are called can know God through him.

In the same manner, Christ the crucified is also the means through which the believers receive righteousness, sanctification, and redemption. Thus, no one can boast, but if one must, let such person boast in the Lord for what God has done and given him through Christ.

In 1 Corinthians 2:1–5, Paul calls on the Corinthian believers as his witnesses that his proclamation of the gospel did not rely on human persuasiveness to convince them but on the power of the Spirit of God manifested in his weakness so that their faith might not rest on wisdom of the world but on the power of God. His method is a manifestation that the message of the cross is in itself the power of God so it does not need human persuasiveness to convict people and lead them to a life of faith in Christ.

Paul reveals that God can only be known through the Spirit of God. Again, Paul exposes the limitation of the wisdom of the world in knowing the wisdom of God. The crucifixion proves that the rulers of this age did not understand the wisdom of God because if they did, they would not have crucified him. They did not understand Christ is God's agent for the salvation of humanity. Why? Paul explains these things are beyond the grasp of the wisdom of the world. It belongs to God and unless God reveals it through the Spirit to those he calls his own and those who love him it cannot be known. Thus, the spiritual person is the one understands the wisdom of God because the Spirit of God reveals it to him.

Paul's integrated discussion of wisdom and boasting shows that the boastings and quarreling in the church do not attest to a life of wisdom even though they have already received the proclamation of the cross. As people of God, they are supposed to demonstrate a life that conforms to the life of a believer who has the Spirit of God. But their quarreling proves otherwise. Their quarreling shows they are not people of the wisdom of God but people of the wisdom of the world. Thus, they boast about their preferred missionary worker, criticize the other, and quarrel against each other. They failed to see that their missionary workers are God's servants. The missionary workers are not in competition with each other so there is no reason for the Corinthian believers to even compare them with one another.

Finally, God has designed that the way for people to be wise is to embrace the wisdom of God. What the wisdom of the world calls foolishness actually makes an individual truly wise. As people of the wisdom of God, they must cease from boasting about their preferred missionary worker and act as if he exclusively belongs to their house churches. On the contrary, the missionary workers of Corinth belong to the entire church so there is no reason to favor the one and reject the other.

4.2 Paul's Wisdom Teaching and Its Relation to the Corinthian Problems in 1 Corinthians 1–4

In dealing with the problem of division in the Corinthian church in 1 Corinthians 1–4, Paul did not spend an extensive discourse proportional to the gravity of the problem albeit it was a church-wide threat. Rather he takes a quick yet strong appeal to modify the problem of division then introduced a concept that at first glance looks immaterial to the exigency at hand. In this brief discussion on the problem of division he begins with an appeal of unity introduced by the word παρακαλῶ in 1 Corinthians 1:10. He also alludes to the fact that baptism may have contributed to the quarreling in the church. After a quick transition in 1:17 he takes a long pause from his discussion on the problem of division then navigates through a long discourse of his wisdom teaching interspersed with his discussion of the boastings of the Corinthian believers that causes quarreling among them before resuming to his final appeal to imitate him indicated with the word παρακαλῶ again in 4:16, thereby closing the loop of his discourse. With this approach, Paul seems to indicate that he is addressing more than one problem.[64] Paul sees

---

64. Pogoloff, *Logos and Sophia*, 119.

a web of problems that are interconnected causing the relationship of the Corinthian believers to slowly fall apart.

An overview of Paul's discourse shows the probable connection of the problems of division, wisdom, and boasting. Paul deliberated on the problem of division from 1:10–17. In 1:18–3:23 Paul's wisdom teaching comes to expression. Paul alludes to the misconception of the Corinthian believers about wisdom where they connect rhetorical ability to being wise. In response, he seeks to redefine their understanding of wisdom by pointing them to the crucified Christ and the role of the Spirit of God in the revelation. That is, true wisdom is found in Christ the wisdom of God that is revealed through the Spirit of God to those who believe. Thus, their boastings about themselves and their leaders manifest a life devoid of spirituality, a false sense of superiority, and a wisdom that causes them to boast and criticize others. Then, in 4:1–21 Paul closes the discussion on boasting and division with an appeal of unity towards the end.[65]

It is my contention that Paul's wisdom teaching is his response, if not, solution to help address the three problems in the Corinthian church in 1 Corinthians 1–4. In this section, I argue that the problem of division is related to the problem of boasting and rooted in the problem of wisdom. Hence, Paul's response to the three problems in the Corinthian church is to instruct them properly about the wisdom of God. In view of this, this section establishes the relationship of Paul's wisdom teaching first to the problem of wisdom, the root of the problems of the Corinthian church, then connects it to the problem of boasting which is the cause of the problem of division.

4.2.1 Paul's Wisdom Teaching and the Problem of Wisdom

The problem of wisdom is induced by the Corinthian believers' interest in wisdom and rhetoric as a result of the influence of the sophistic practices in the first century and perhaps that of Apollos when he visited the church few years earlier. Apollos was eloquent in speech and knowledgeable with the Scriptures (Acts 18:24–25). Paul, on the other hand, as indicated in his manifestations that he did not rely on the use of persuasive speech in the proclamation of the gospel, is being compared to Apollos and criticized for his lack of rhetorical skills (1 Cor 2:15). During the first century, rhetoric

---

65. Cf. Frestadius, "Spirit and Wisdom," 52–70.

was popular and highly patronized among the wealthy and powerful. So, the wealthy church patrons who are interested in rhetoric are the ones who preferred Apollos and supported him. If so, they along with their respective house churches are the ones criticizing Paul for his lack of rhetoric (1 Cor 2:1–5; 3:15; 4:1–5).

As such, the slogans in 1 Corinthians 1:12, Ἐγὼ μέν εἰμι Παύλου, Ἐγὼ δὲ Ἀπολλῶ, Ἐγὼ δὲ Κηφᾶ, Ἐγὼ δὲ Χριστοῦ, are perhaps influenced by the sophistic-like behavior of the first-century disciples who have pledged loyalty to their sophists and are engaged in disparaging other disciples and sophists. As indicated by Paul's statement in 1 Corinthians 3:3, their conduct reflects the conduct of mere humans. Corinthian believers are criticizing one another. They are led by their respective church patrons who seemed to consider themselves as disciples of their preferred missionary like the eloquent Apollos while others whom Paul baptized consider themselves as disciples of Paul.

In view of Paul's wisdom teaching, Paul asserts that the pursuit of the wisdom of the world is futile. It is because what people consider as a superior wisdom is actually inferior compared to the wisdom of God. Though the wisdom of the world is known for its eloquence and knowledge and highly esteemed and pursued by humans, it failed to know and understand the wisdom God. To people it is foolishness. In 1 Corinthians 1:20 Paul shows that the wise man, scribe, and the debater of this age could not understand the wisdom of God through the wisdom of the world. This points to an important fact that there's nothing to boast about with respect to the wisdom of the world. More importantly, it is not a worthy pursuit. Thus, they must realign their pursuit to the wisdom of God who gives them righteousness, holiness, and sanctification. That is, in view of the quarreling in the church they need to reevaluate whether their actions reflect the wisdom of the world or the wisdom of God and realign themselves to reflect that they are a people of the wisdom of God.

When Paul says, "not many of you were wise, powerful, and noble," he is making a statement that, although many of the Corinthian believers are not wise, powerful, and noble according to the standards of the wisdom of the world, God made them understand the message of the cross, as later explained by Paul in 2:6–16, through the revelation of the Spirit of God. In this sense because their understanding of the message of the cross was not achieved through the wisdom of the world none of them can boast about it before men or before God.

In conjunction with his discussion on wisdom, Paul also clarifies that there is no basis to criticize him about the nature of his preaching because he made a conscious decision not to rely on human persuasiveness in order that their response to the gospel would not be motivated as well as influenced by the persuasiveness of his speech but by the power of God that is at work through the Spirit of God. He made a conscious choice to distance himself from the usual manner of public speaking so that their faith would not rest on the wisdom of people but on the wisdom of God. In effect, Paul is also saying that he should not be categorized with these other public speakers or rhetors because the proclamation of the gospel must be accomplished through the divine work of God. It also implies then that when Paul asserts that he and Apollos are co-workers he is in effect saying that just like him Apollos did not preach the gospel using human persuasion though he was known to be eloquent. That is, when some of them heard the gospel through Apollos and received it, it was not because Apollos was eloquent but because the power of God was at work in their lives through the Spirit of God.

Paul also alludes to their tendency of examining the worth of their leaders especially in relation to their rhetorical ability and boast about them. Paul explains that he and Apollos are servants of the Lord. They are both doing the same work of God and though they may differ in their roles yet they are one, as Paul makes it explicit in 1 Corinthians 3:9, "Now he who plants and he who waters are one." More importantly, none of them should be attributed any honor for the growth in the church because it is God who causes the growth. So, since they are mere servants of God who have no inherent power to cause growth, there is no reason to boast about any of them.

Some of the Corinthian believers think they are wise but Paul refutes them by showing their claim is based on a false premise (1 Cor 3:18–20). Paul raises two things here. First, he warns them about not being deceived into thinking that they are already wise or can become wise based on the standards of the wisdom of the world. Before God, this kind of wisdom is foolishness so they will not be considered wise at all. Second, if they want to be wise they must embrace and pursue the wisdom of God that they consider foolishness. On being wise, Paul urges the believers to stop boasting about their missionary workers because a divisive spirit is not a proof of wisdom but of foolishness.

This is a call to cease from pursuing the wisdom of the world because its manifestations in the church, as well as the boastings and quarreling, are damaging to the unity of the body. Paul further connects the problem of wisdom to the problem of boasting in 1 Corinthians 3.

4.2.2 Paul's Wisdom Teaching and the Problem of Boasting

From the outset, Paul introduces the problem of boasting through the slogans in 1 Corinthians 1:12 "I am of Paul," "I of Apollos," "I of Cephas," and "I of Christ." The emphasis of the "I" indicates that this boasting is motivated by the desire to elevate oneself. That is, their boasting about their preferred missionary worker is a veiled approach to boast about themselves. After addressing the problem of wisdom in 1 Corinthians 1–3, Paul proceeds to address the problem of boasting 1 Corinthians 3.

In 1 Corinthians 3:1–9 the Corinthian believers were envious and jealous against other groups who were taking pride about who baptized them or about their preferred missionary worker's rhetorical ability and achievements in the ministry. So, Paul unleashes a polemic against their jealousy and quarreling that do not reflect the conduct of spiritual people. Paul explains that he and Apollos are co-workers in the Lord who have different roles but as both servants of Christ they are one. Thus, there is no quarrel or envy between them. In fact, there is no reason to boast about any of them because it was God who caused the growth in the church.

In this concluding section of 1 Corinthians 3, Paul reminds the Corinthian believers that they should not allow their boasting about their missionary workers to cause division among the believers because no missionary worker exclusively belongs to one household congregation but all the missionary workers belong to the entire Corinthians congregation. Consequently, everyone belongs to Christ, the wisdom of God. So then, since they all belong to Christ they are one and there must be no boasting among them. They must not allow their boastings to destroy the unity of the body of Christ.

Following through this line of thought, in 4:1–5 Paul stresses that he and other missionary workers must be treated as co-workers, servants of Christ and people who belong to God just as everyone is. He declares that he is not bothered being examined by them. In fact, he does not examine himself because after all, it is God who examines him. Paul's rhetorical strategy here is his final attempt to quell the divisive conduct of the Corinthian believers by avowing to his trustworthiness as servant of Christ and steward of God's mysteries so that they will be moved to act upon the exigencies and resolve to come together in unity.

Paul exhorts the Corinthian believers not to judge others because whether one person or missionary worker deserves to be honored in this manner or not it is the Lord who can truly judge when he returns at the appointed time. In the meantime, they must not judge others so that they will not boast about their preferred missionary worker and disparage others. Their critical spirit is detrimental to the unity of the church. This is the reason why there are quarrels and boasting among them.

Further, in 4:6 Paul refers to pride as being puffed up. By being puffed up it means they have regarded themselves and their missionary workers beyond who they really are. As such, they have developed a superior attitude over others toward others and perhaps over Paul.

In 1 Corinthians 4:7 Paul confronts their false sense of superiority. Earlier in 4:1–5 Paul lays down his trustworthiness in light of the fact that God examines him. So now he challenges their claims: "For who regards you as superior? What do you have that you did not receive? And if you did receive it, why do you boast as if you had not received it?"

Paul's wisdom concept addresses not only the problem of wisdom but also the problem of boasting. In the course of refuting the Corinthian's wrong understanding of wisdom, Paul also exposes the weakness of their boasting. Altogether, Paul argues their pursuit of wisdom is futile and their boasting is baseless. In effect Paul argues that if they pursue the wisdom of God, they will not boast anymore and then there is no more reason to be divided.

Boasting about their leaders reflects the boasting of the world. That is, boasting about their leaders stands parallel to how the world measures one person and boasts about it. The people around that time look at the sophists as the ultimate source of wisdom and they boast about somebody. This is human boasting. If this is human boasting, then it shows they do not have the Spirit of God, which means they do not have the wisdom of God. If they do not have wisdom of God, then they're just like the people in their time who are enamored to the wisdom of the world. Is this true? It is not. They are God's people through the Christ crucified. Thus, they have the Spirit of God. Since they have the Spirit of God they must stop boasting about their missionary workers because it is causing disunity. If their conduct is causing disunity, it does not reflect the implication of the message of the cross where those who have the wisdom of God are called to live their lives in unity as a testament that they are spiritual people. And as spiritual people who have received the divine inheritance of righteousness, sanctification, and redemption, there is only one way to boast. That is to boast in the Lord who has given them true wisdom, the wisdom of God. Not because they are wise, powerful, and noble or people of eloquence or people who have achieved the wisdom of the world but people who believe that the message of the cross is the wisdom of God.

In every sense, their boasting about their preferred missionary worker has sparked quarreling among them that lead to division. Paul addresses their boasting to avoid the imminent danger of being completely divided into separate communities of congregations that are not only independently existing but also hostile to one another.

4.2.3 Paul's Wisdom Teaching and the Problem of Division

We have already established the relationship of wisdom to the problem of boasting as well as how their boastings have caused quarrels among them that lead to division.

The problem of division is marked by the mention of σχίσματα in 1 Corinthians 1:10. What are some factors that contributed to the quarreling?

The church setting in the early days of the Corinthian church was different from most of the churches these days. Unlike today where an entire congregation gathers in one place for worship the Corinthian congregations are hosted weekly in different homes of the church patrons (wealthy converts). As the church grows other houses of the church patrons are made available like the houses of Justus, Gaius, Crispus, and Stephanas to accommodate the growing congregation. Occasionally, the entire congregation would gather at the house of Gaius for worship but most of the time they meet separately in different homes of the patrons. How did they maintain unity as household churches? We can deduce from Paul's appeal in 1 Corinthians 1:10 that their basis of unity is in having the same mind and intention. They may be meeting in separate groups being hosted in different homes weekly but they are united because they are in one mind and intention.

However, quarrels erupt among the different house churches. The special bond that exists between the patron and missionary workers who would frequently visit this house or church gathering probably instigates the quarreling.

They begin to develop a sense of loyalty to their preferred missionary worker who is, in all probability, the one who baptizes members of the household church. Since there are many poor people in the church who belong to the lower class it is understandable that they become economically dependent to the church patrons. In this manner it is unavoidable that these people also come alongside the patron and join them in boasting about the patron's preferred missionary worker and criticize the other. As such, it is safe to assume that the quarrels between house churches are primarily instigated by the patrons of different household gatherings whom Paul identifies as the wise, powerful, and noble people in 1 Corinthians 1:26 together with the other members of the congregation of the house churches especially those who were economically dependent to their patrons.

The Corinthian believers think they are wise (1 Cor 3:18) but their conduct is dividing the church. Their boasting and quarreling do not reflect the conduct of spiritual people who have the wisdom of God. So, Paul calls on them to seek the wisdom of God and cease from boasting which causes quarreling that leads to division. Since all belongs to Christ, the wisdom of God, then, there is no reason to be divided anymore.

4.3 Summary

Paul's wisdom teaching addresses the root cause of the problems in the church, the problem of wisdom. Paul modifies the faulty understanding of wisdom. That is, they thought the wisdom of the world makes them wise but the opposite is true. As shown by their conduct, they are foolish. They gained a false sense of superiority that causes them to boast about themselves and their preferred missionary worker. As a result, their foolishness is manifested in their boastings and quarreling that leads to division. Paul's wisdom teaching seeks to realign and redefine them into behaving as people of the wisdom of God as they really are. The wisdom of God gives righteousness, holiness and redemption. As such, they must cease from boasting about themselves, boasting about Apollos or Paul and criticizing Paul for his lack of rhetoric. Their boasting is divisive and it betrays the implication of the message of the cross that unites those who believe whether Jews or Greeks, eloquent or not, wise, noble, powerful or not. As people of the wisdom of God, they can choose to be in one mind and intention to preserve the unity of the body.

CHAPTER 5

Conclusion

The situation in the Corinthian church in 1 Corinthians 1–4 has three interrelated exigencies: the problems of division, boasting, and wisdom. The problem of division is evident by the quarreling among the Corinthian believers over their missionary workers. It is likely that these quarrels are carried on with the leadership of the household patrons whom Paul identifies in 1 Corinthians 1:26 and 4:10 as wise, powerful, or strong, and noble or honorable along with the congregation in their respective house churches. The quarreling in the church existed between two groups, the Paul group and the Apollos group. In 1 Corinthians 1:12, Paul seems to refer to four groups as evident by the slogans. However, Paul refers to Paul and Apollos only whenever he discusses the exigencies in 1 Corinthians 1–4 particularly in 3:4–5 when he asks, "For when one says, 'I am of Paul,' and another says, 'I am of Apollos,' are you not mere men? What then is Apollos? And What is Paul?" and in 4:6 when he says, "Now these things brothers, I applied to myself and Apollos on your account in order that in us you may learn not to exceed what is written, in order that no one becomes arrogant on behalf of one against another." He did not mention or connect the Cephas and Christ groups to any of the exigencies in the church. The Corinthian believers were quarreling because they were boasting about Paul and Apollos. Thus, the problem of division is occasioned by the problem of boasting. Those who prefer Apollos are boasting about the rhetorical skills of Apollos while at the same time criticizing Paul. Those who prefer Paul are also boasting about his achievements as the founder of the church in an attempt to assuage the criticisms hurled against Paul.

Paul's discussion on boasting is interspersed with his discussion on the problem of wisdom. Paul emphasizes the futility of the wisdom of the world and points out that the proper way of boasting is in boasting about God who has given them the wisdom of God and has caused the growth in the church, not about their missionary workers who are God's servants. Also, Paul exhorts the Corinthian believers not to be deceived into thinking they are wise. They think they are wise. However, their evaluation of themselves as wise is based on a false sense of superiority. This false sense of superiority leads them to boast about themselves and the missionary workers as well as criticize others including their missionary workers.

Paul's integrated discussion of wisdom and boasting shows that the boastings and quarreling in the church do not attest to a life of wisdom despite the fact that they have already received the proclamation of the cross. As people of God, they are supposed to demonstrate a life that conforms to the life of a believer who has the Spirit of God. But their quarreling proves otherwise. Their quarreling shows they are not people of the wisdom of God but people of the wisdom of the world. Thus, they boast about their preferred missionary worker, criticize the other, and quarrel against each other. Paul reiterates that their boasting has no basis because they do not belong to their missionary workers. Instead, their missionary workers belong to all of them and all of them belong to Christ.

In order to modify the exigency in the Corinthian church, Paul teaches them his wisdom teaching. Paul presents his wisdom teaching in view of how God reveals himself so that people may know him. It is God's design that the wise man, the scribe, and the debater of this age, even if they claim to possess a superior wisdom, they cannot know God unless God chooses to reveal himself to them through the Holy Spirit.

Paul asserts that Christ is the "power of God and wisdom of God." Christ, being the power of God, is the means by which people can know God. Christ, being the wisdom of God, is the embodiment of the wisdom of God and those who believe and those who are called can know God through him. In the same manner, Christ the crucified is also the means through which the believers receive righteousness, sanctification, and redemption. Thus, no one can boast, but if one has to, let such person boast in the Lord for what God has done and given him through Christ.

In conclusion, the problem of division is caused by the problem of boasting and rooted in the problem of wisdom. Paul's wisdom teaching addresses the root cause of the exigencies in the church, the problem of wisdom. Paul seeks to modify their faulty understanding of wisdom and teaches them they can only become wise by embracing Christ, the wisdom of God, revealed through the Holy Spirit. Wisdom belongs to God and unless he reveals it through the Spirit to those he calls his own and those who love him wisdom cannot be known. The spiritual person is the one who understands the wisdom of God because the Spirit of God reveals it to him. They claim to be wise but Paul points out that their quarreling in the church shows they are foolish and unspiritual. In addition, their false sense of superiority causes them to boast about themselves and their preferred missionary worker. Paul's wisdom teaching seeks to redefine their understanding of who they are, so that they behave as they really are – people of the wisdom of God. As such, they must stop boasting about themselves, Apollos, and Paul. Their boasting is divisive and it betrays the implication of the message of the cross that unites those who believe whether Jews or Greeks, eloquent or not, wise, noble, powerful or not.

Thus, as people of the wisdom of God, they must seek Christ and choose to be in one mind and intention to keep the unity of the body of Christ. Then, the boasting ceases. When the boasting ceases, there will be no quarreling and the Corinthian believers may live in the same mind and same purpose.

5.1 Contribution of the Study

This study offers three contributions to the Pauline studies particularly for 1 Corinthians 1–4. First, it establishes the connection between Paul's wisdom teaching and the problems in the Corinthian church, namely, division, boasting, and wisdom. The lack of scholarship dedicated to studying the relationship of Paul's wisdom teaching to the problems in 1 Corinthians 1–4 called for an analysis on Paul's response to the rhetorical situation in the Corinthian church. Second, it explains how the three problems are interrelated. This area provides an answer to the allusions of several authors on the possible connections of the three problems as evidenced by the manner in which Paul interspersed his arguments in addressing the problems of division, boasting, and wisdom. Third, it demonstrates that the quarreling in the Corinthian church exists only between the Paul group and the Apollos group. Apart from 1 Corinthians 1:12, there is no mention of the four groups, namely, the Paul group, Apollos group, Cephas group, and Christ group, elsewhere in 1 Corinthians. This lack of reference to the four groups especially in relation to the problems in 1 Corinthians 1–4, necessitated an analysis of Paul's rhetorical purpose of mentioning the slogan in 1 Corinthians 1:12 in relation to the problems in 1 Corinthians 1–4.

5.2 Relevance of the Study to the Context of the Christian Churches in the Philippines

This study also offers relevant ideas to the context of the Christian churches in the Philippines especially on the issue of division. It is a common knowledge that many churches have been divided due to conflicts among members of the church. These conflicts have caused rifts in many relationships and because they could not agree anymore, some members have opted to leave the church and formed another congregation.[1] At the surface level, these conflicts are caused by disagreements over financial matters, church administration, and sometimes even over non-essential matters. However, at the deeper level, the real issue revolves around the members' understanding of their relationship with Christ. How does their faith in Christ affect their relationship with one another and conduct in the church? People claim they are followers of Christ but their conduct in the church speaks otherwise. People say they are spiritually mature but many are consumed by their anger, pride, unforgiving spirit, stubborn spirit, and more. These manifestations do not reflect the attitude and life of a follower of Christ. If only Christians live their lives as true followers of Christ, these conflicts would have been resolved. It would not have resulted to church divisions. The church needs to be reminded that their anger, pride, unforgiving spirit, stubbornness, and others betray the implication of the message of the cross that calls every believer to be in the same mind and intention to keep the unity of the body of Christ.

5.3 Areas of Further Research

This study evokes several questions for further research. Through a rhetorical analysis, this study has demonstrated the relevance of Paul's wisdom teaching to the problems in 1 Corinthians 1–4. Since the Corinthian believers sent

---

1. For one particular Filipino example see the discussion in Mabborang, "Causes and Effects of Division."

Paul a letter to inquire from him about some issues in the church, how does Paul's wisdom teaching relate to the problems mentioned in the letter sent through Stephanas, Fortunatus and Achaicus? That is, with a broader study of rhetorical analysis of 1 Corinthians, can Paul's wisdom teaching provide a lens for seeing how it may be relevant to the other problems mentioned in 1 Corinthians? For example, in 1 Corinthians 5 Paul confronts the fornication in the church, which the church believers tolerated. Paul accuses them of becoming arrogant. How is the arrogant attitude of the Corinthian believers in 1 Corinthians 5 similar or different from the problems in 1 Corinthians 1–4? More importantly, how does Paul's wisdom teaching fit into the situation? Is it possible that the arrogant attitude of the believers is related to their faulty understanding of what it means to be wise as well as a faulty understanding of their relationship with Christ? In another situation, Paul mentions of σχίσματα in 1 Corinthians 11. Again, how does Paul's wisdom teaching relate to the problem of division in 1 Corinthians 11? Similarly, how does Paul's response to the problems in 1 Corinthians 1–4 fit into his overall rhetorical argument in 1 Corinthians? Also, as I have argued that the quarrel exists between the Paul and Apollos groups, perhaps an investigation can be explored on how the quarreling may have escalated or subsided after Paul wrote the letter to the Corinthian believers. How did Paul's letter affect the quarreling in the church after they have read it? Obviously, the Corinthian believers did not expect that Paul's letter would contain a message addressing the problems of division, boasting, and wisdom. How might have the Corinthian believers especially those who belong to the Paul and Apollos groups reacted upon hearing the unexpected message of Paul on this matter?

Bibliography

Primary Sources

Aristotle. *Art of Rhetoric*. Translated by J. H. Freese. Loeb Classical Library 193. Cambridge, MA: Harvard University Press, 1926.

Cicero. *De Inventione*; *De Optimo Genere Oratorum*; *Topica*. Translated by H. M. Hubbell. Loeb Classical Library 386. Cambridge, MA: Harvard University Press, 1949.

———. *De Oratore I–II*. Translated by E. W. Sutton and H. Rackham. Loeb Classical Library 348. Cambridge, MA: Harvard University Press, 1942.

———. *Tusculan Disputations*. Translated by J. E. King. Loeb Classical Library 141. Cambridge, MA: Harvard University Press, 1927.

Dio Chrysostom. *Discourses 1–11*. Translated by J. W. Cohoon. Loeb Classical Library 257. Cambridge, MA: Harvard University Press, 1932.

———. *Discourses 37–60*. Translated by H. Lamar Crosby. Loeb Classical Library 376. Cambridge, MA: Harvard University Press, 1946.

Philo. Translated by F. H. Colson and G. H. Whitaker. 10 vols. Loeb Classical Library. Cambridge, MA: Harvard University Press, 1929–62.

Philostratus, Eunapius. *The Lives of the Sophists*. Translated by Wilmer Cave Wright. Loeb Classical Library 134. London: Heinemann, 1922.

Quintilian. *Institutio Oratoria. Volume II: Books 3–4*. Translated by H. E. Butler. Loeb Classical Library 125. London: William Heinemann, 1920.

Strabo. *Geography, Volume IV: Books 8–9*. Translated by Horace Leonard Jones. Loeb Classical Library 196. Cambridge, MA: Harvard University Press, 1927.

Articles and Books

Adams, Edward, and David G. Horrell, eds. *Christianity at Corinth: The Quest for the Pauline Church*. Louisville, KY: Westminster John Knox, 2004.

Askani, Hans-Christoph. "The Paradox of Faith." In *The Wisdom and Foolishness of God: First Corinthians 1–2 in Theological Exploration*, edited by Christophe Chalamet and Hans-Christoph Askani, 341–58. Minneapolis, MN: Fortress, 2015.

Baird, William. "Among the Mature: The Idea of Wisdom in 1 Corinthians 2:6." *Interpretation* 13 (1959): 425–32.

———. "'One Against the Other': Intra-church Conflict in 1 Corinthians." In *The Conversation Continues: Studies Paul and John in Honor of J. Louis Martyn*, edited by R. T. Fortna and B. Gaventa, 116–36. Nashville, TN: Abingdon, 1990.

Barbour, Robin S. "Wisdom and the Cross in 1 Corinthians 1 and 2." In *Theologia Crucis – Signum Crucis: Festschrift fur Erich Dinkler zum 70 Geburtstag*, edited by C. Andresen and G. Klein, 57–71. Tübingen: Mohr Siebeck, 1979.

Barclay, John M. G. "Crucifixion as Wisdom: Exploring the Ideology of a Disreputable Social Movement." In *The Wisdom and Foolishness of God: First Corinthians 1–2 in Theological Exploration*, edited by Christophe Chalamet and Hans-Christoph Askani, 1–20. Minneapolis, MN: Fortress, 2015.

———. *Pauline Churches and Diaspora Jews*. Tübingen: Mohr Siebeck, 2011.

Barnett, Paul W. *The Corinthian Question: Why Did the Church Oppose Paul*. Nottingham: Apollos, 2011.

Barrett, Charles Kingsley. *A Commentary on the First Epistle to the Corinthians*. Black's New Testament Commentary. Peabody, MA: Hendrickson, 1968.

Barton, George A. "Some Influences of Apollos in the New Testament, I." *Journal of Biblical Literature* 43, no. 1/2 (1924): 207–23.

Bauer, W. *A Greek-English Lexicon of the New Testament and Other Early Christian Literature*. Revised and edited by Frederick William Danker. 3rd ed. Chicago, IL: University of Chicago Press, 2000.

Baur, F. C. *Paul the Apostle of Jesus Christ, His Life and Work, His Epistle and Teachings*. Vol. 1. Peabody, MA: Hendrickson, 2003. Reprinted in one volume from the original two-volume English edition of F. C. Baur. *Paul the Apostle of Jesus Christ, His Life and Work, His Epistle and His Doctrine: A Contribution to a Critical History of Primitive Christianity*. London: Williams & Norgate, 1873–1875.

———. "The Two Epistles to the Corinthians." In *Christianity at Corinth: The Quest for the Pauline Church*, edited by Edward Adams and David G. Horrell, 51–60. Louisville, KY: Westminster John Knox, 2004.

Betz, Hans Dieter. "The Literary Composition and Function of Paul's Letter to the Galatians." *New Testament Studies* 21, no. 3 (1975): 353–79.

Beaudean, John William, Jr. *Paul's Theology of Preaching*. National Association of Baptist Professors of Religion Dissertation Series 6. Macon, GA: Mercer University Press, 1988.

Bitner, Bradley J. *Paul's Political Strategy in 1 Corinthians 1–4: Constitution and Covenant*. Society for New Testament Studies Monograph Series 163. New York, NY: Cambridge University Press, 2015.

Bitzer, Lloyd F. "The Rhetorical Situation." *Philosophy and Rhetoric* 1, no. 1 (1968): 1–14.

Bookidis, Nancy. "Religion in Corinth: 146 B.C.E. to 100 C.E." In *Urban Religion in Roman Corinth: Interdisciplinary Approaches*, edited by Daniel N. Schowalter and Steven J. Friesen, 141–64. Harvard Theological Studies 53. Cambridge, MA: Harvard University Press, 2005.

Bowersock, G. W. *Greek Sophists in the Roman Empire*. Oxford: Clarendon, 1969.

Brinton, Alan. "Situation in the Theory of Rhetoric." *Philosophy and Rhetoric* 14, no. 4 (1981): 234–48.

Brookins, Timothy A. *Corinthian Wisdom, Stoic Philosophy, and the Ancient Economy*. Society for New Testament Studies Monograph Series 159. New York, NY: Cambridge University Press, 2014.

———. "The Wise Corinthians: Their Stoic Education and Outlook." *The Journal of Theological Studies* 62, no. 1 (2011): 51–76.

Broneer, Oscar. "The Apostle Paul and the Isthmian Games." *The Biblical Archaeologist* 25, no. 1 (1962): 1–31.

Burke, Trevor. "Paul's Role as 'Father' to His Corinthian 'Children' in Socio-Historical Context (1 Corinthians 4:14–21)." In *Paul and the Corinthians: Studies on a Community in Conflict: Essays in Honour of Margaret Thrall*, edited by Trevor J. Burke and J. Keith Elliott, 95–114. Leiden: Brill, 2003.

Castelli, Elizabeth A. *Imitating Paul: A Discourse of Power*. Louisville, KY: Westminster John Knox, 1991.

Chow, John K. *Patronage and Power: A Study of Social Networks in Corinth*. Journal for the Study of the New Testament Supplement Series 75. Sheffield: Sheffield Academic, 1992.

Ciampa, Roy E., and Brian S. Rosner. *The First Letter to the Corinthians*. Pillar New Testament Commentary. Grand Rapids, MI: Eerdmans, 2010.

Clarke, Andrew D. *Secular and Christian Leadership in Corinth: A Socio-Historical and Exegetical Study of 1 Corinthians 1–6*. Leiden: Brill, 1993.

Collins, Raymond F. *First Corinthians*. Edited by D. J. Harrington. Sacra Pagina 7. Collegeville, MN: Liturgical Press, 1999.

Conzelmann, Hans. *1 Corinthians: A Commentary on the First Epistle to the Corinthians*. Hermenia Series. Philadelphia, PA: Fortress, 1975.

Dahl, Nils A. "Paul and the Church at Corinth According to 1 Corinthians 1:10–4:21." In *Christian History and Interpretation Studies Presented to John Knox*, edited by W. R. Farmer, C. F. D. Moule, and R. R. Niebuhr, 313–35. Cambridge: Cambridge University Press, 1967.

———. "Paul and the Church at Corinth According to 1 Corinthians 1:10–4:21." In *Studies in Paul: Theology of the Early Christian Mission*, 40–61. Minneapolis, MN: Augsburg, 1977.

Davis, James A. *Wisdom and Spirit: An Investigation of 1 Corinthians 1.18–3.20 against the Background of Jewish Sapiential Traditions in the Greco-Roman Period*. Lanham, MD: University Press of America, 1984.

Ebert, Daniel J., IV. *Wisdom Christology: How Jesus Becomes God's Wisdom for Us*. Phillipsburg, NJ: P&R, 2011.

Elliott, John H. *What Is Social Scientific Criticism?* Minneapolis, MN: Fortress, 1993.

Ellis, E. Earle. *Prophecy and Hermeneutic in Early Christianity*. Grand Rapids, MI: Eerdmans, 1978.

Engels, Donald. *Roman Corinth: An Alternative Model for the Classic Society*. Chicago, IL: University of Chicago Press, 1990.

Ehrensperger, Kathy. *Paul and the Dynamics of Power: Communication and Interaction in the Early Christ-Movement*. Library of New Testament Studies 325. New York, NY: T&T Clark, 2007.

Finley, Moses I. *The Ancient Economy*. Berkeley, CA: University of California Press, 1973.

Filson, Floyd V. "The Significance of the Early House Churches." *Journal of Biblical Literature* 58, no. 2 (1939): 105–12.

Fiorenza, Elisabeth Schüssler. "Rhetorical Situation and Historical Reconstruction in I Corinthians." *New Testament Studies* 33, no. 3 (1987): 386–403.

Fitzmyer, Joseph A. *First Corinthians*. The Anchor Yale Bible 32. New Haven, CT: Yale University Press. 2008.

Fee, Gordon. *The First Epistle to the Corinthians*. New International Commentary of the New Testament. Grand Rapids, MI: Eerdmans, 1987.

Fotopoulos, John. "1 Corinthians." In *The Blackwell Companion to the New Testament*, edited by David E. Aune, 413–33. Chichester: Wiley-Blackwell, 2010.

Francis, J. "'As Babes in Christ' – Some Proposals Regarding 1 Corinthians 3:1–3." *Journal for the Study of the New Testament* 2, no. 7 (1980): 41–60.

Frestadius, Simo. "The Spirit and Wisdom in 1 Corinthians 2:1–13." *Journal of Biblical and Pneumatological Research* 3 (2011): 52–70.

Funk, Robert W. *Language, Hermeneutic and Word of God: The Problem of Language in the New Testament and Contemporary Theology*. New York, NY: Harper and Row, 1966.

Gager, John G. *Kingdom and Community: The Social World of Early Christianity*. Englewood Cliffs, NJ: Prentice-Hall, 1975.

———. "Social Description and Sociological Explanation in the Study of Early Christianity: A Review Essay." In *The Bible and Liberation: Political and Social*

Hermeneutics, edited by Norman K. Gottwald, 428–40. Maryknoll, NY: Orbis Books, 1984.

Garland, David E. *1 Corinthians*. Baker Exegetical Commentary on the New Testament. Grand Rapids, MI: Baker Academic, 2003.

Garnsey, Peter, and Richard Saller. *The Roman Empire: Economy, Society and Culture*. Berkeley, CA: University of California Press, 1987.

Given, Mark. *Paul's True Rhetoric: Ambiguity, Cunning, and Deception in Greece and Rome*. Harrisbugh, PA: Trinity Press International, 2001.

Goodrich, John K. *Paul as an Administrator of God in 1 Corinthians*. Society of New Testament Studies Monograph Series 152. Cambridge: Cambridge University Press, 2012.

Gottwald, Norman K. "Sociological Methods in Biblical Research and Contemporary Peace Studies." *American Baptist Quarterly* 2 (1983): 142–56.

Green, Donald E. "The Folly of the Cross." *The Master's Seminary Journal* 15, no. 1 (2004): 59–69.

Grindheim, Sigurd. "Wisdom for the Perfect: Paul's Challenge to the Corinthian Church (1 Corinthians 2:6–16)." *Journal of Biblical Literature* 121, no. 4 (2002): 689–709.

Grosheide, F. W. *Commentary on the First Epistle to the Corinthians*. New International Commentary of the New Testament. Grand Rapids, MI: Eerdmans, 1979.

Hall, David R. "A Disguise for the Wise: ΜΕΤΑΣΧΗΜΑΤΙΣΜΟΣ in 1 Corinthians 4:6." *New Testament Studies* 40, no. 1 (1994): 143–49.

Hays, Richard B. "Wisdom According to Paul." In *Where Shall Wisdom Be Found: Wisdom in the Bible, the Church and the Contemporary World*, edited by Stephen C. Barton, 111–124. Edinburgh: T&T Clark, 1999.

Heil, John Paul. *The Rhetorical Role of Scripture in 1 Corinthians*. Studies in Biblical Literature 15. Atlanta, GA: Society of Biblical Literature, 2005.

Hendrix, Holland. "Benefactor/Patron Networks in the Urban Environment: Evidence from Thessalonica." *Semeia* 56 (1991): 39–58.

Holland, Glenn. "Paul's Use of Irony as a Rhetorical Technique." In *The Rhetorical Analysis of Scripture: Essays from 1995 London Conference*, edited by S. E. Porter and T. H. Olbricht, 234–48. Journal for the Study of the New Testament Supplement Series 146. Sheffield: Sheffield Academic, 1997.

Hooker, Morna D. "'Beyond the Things Which Are Written': An Examination of 1 Cor. IV:6." *New Testament Studies* 10, no. 1 (1963): 127–32.

Horrell, David G. *The Social Ethos of the Corinthian Correspondence: Interests and Ideology from 1 Corinthians to 1 Clement*. Edinburgh: T&T Clark, 1996.

Horsley, Richard A. "Wisdom of Word and Words of Wisdom in Corinth." *Catholic Biblical Quarterly* 39, no. 2 (1977): 224–39.

Hurd, John Coolidge, Jr. *The Origin of First Corinthians*. Macon, GA: Mercer University Press, 1983.

Hyldahl, Niels. "The Corinthian 'Parties' and the Corinthians Crisis." *Studio Theologica* 45 (1991): 19–32.

Inkelaar, Harm-Jan. *Conflict over Wisdom: The Theme of 1 Corinthians 1–4 Rooted in Scripture*. Leuven: Peeters, 2011.

Jeffers, James S. *The Greco-Roman World of the New Testament Era: Exploring the Background of Early Christianity*. Downers Grove, IL: InterVarsity Press, 1999.

Judge, E. A. "The Early Christians as a Scholastic Community." *Journal of Religious History* 1, no. 1 (1960): 4–15.

———. "The Early Christians as a Scholastic Community: Part II." *Journal of Religious History* 1, no. 3 (1961): 125–37.

———. "Paul's Boasting in relation to Contemporary Professional Practice." *Australian Biblical Review* 16 (1968): 37–50.

———. "The Social Identity of the First Christians: A Question of Method in Religious History." In *Social Distinctives of the Christians in the First Century: Pivotal Essays by E. A. Judge*, edited by David M. Scholer, 117–36. Peabody, MA: Hendrickson, 2008.

———. *Social Pattern of the Christian Groups in the First Century: Some Prolegomena to the Study of the New Testament Ideas of Social Obligation*. London: Tyndale Press, 1960.

Kennedy, George A. *The Art of Persuasion in Greece*. Princeton, NJ: Princeton University Press, 1963.

———. *New Testament Interpretation Through Rhetorical Criticism*. Chapel Hill, NC: University of North Carolina Press, 1984.

Kent, John Harvey. *Corinth: Results of Excavations Conducted by The American School of Classical Studies at Athens. Volume VIII, Part III: The Inscriptions: 1926–1950*. Princeton, NJ: The American School of Classical Studies at Athens, 1966.

Knox, John. *Chapters in the Life of Paul*. Macon, GA: Mercer University Press, 2000.

Koperski, Veronica. "Knowledge of Christ and Knowledge of God in the Corinthians Correspondence." In *The Corinthian Correspondence*, edited by R. Bieringer, 377–96. Leuven: Leuven University Press, 1996.

Kwon, Oh-Young. *1 Corinthians 1–4: Reconstructing Its Social and Rhetorical Situation and Re-Reading It Cross-Culturally for Korean Confucian Christians Today*. Eugene, OR: Wipf & Stock, 2010.

Lampe, Peter. "Paul, Patrons, and Clients." In *Paul in the Greco-Roman World: A Handbook*, edited by J. Paul Sampley, 488–523. Harrisburg, PA: Trinity Press International, 2003.

Lim, Timothy H. "Not in Persuasive Words of Wisdom But in the Demonstration of Spirit and Power." *Novum Testamentum* 29, no. 2 (1987): 137–49.

Litfin, Duane. *St. Paul's Theology of Proclamation: 1 Corinthians 1–4 and Greco-Roman Rhetoric*. Cambridge: Cambridge University Press, 1994.

Longenecker, Richard N. *Galatians*. Word Biblical Commentary 41. Dallas, TX: Word Books, 1990.

Luedemann, Gerd. *Opposition to Paul in Jewish Christianity*. Translated by M. Eugene Boring. Minneapolis, MN: Fortress, 1989.

Mabborang, Francis Dave N. "Causes and Effects of Division of Pentecostal-Evangelical Christian Churches." *Asian Journal of Education and Social Studies* 28 (2022): 26–35.

Malcolm, Matthew R. *Paul and the Rhetoric of Reversal in 1 Corinthians: The Impact of Paul's Gospel on His Macro-Rhetoric*. Society of New Testament Studies Monograph Series 155. Cambridge: Cambridge University Press, 2013.

Malina, Bruce J. "The Social Sciences and Biblical Interpretation." *Interpretation* 36, no. 3 (1982): 229–42.

Malherbe, Abraham J. *Social Aspects of Early Christianity*. Baton Rouge, LA: Louisiana State University, 1977.

Martin, Dale. "Social-Scientific Criticism." In *To Each Its Own Meaning: An Introduction to Biblical Criticisms and Their Application*, edited by Steven L. McKenzie and Stephen R. Haynes, 125–41. Louisville, KY: Westminster John Knox, 1993.

Meeks, Wayne A. *The First Urban Christians: The Social World of Apostle Paul*. New Haven, CT: Yale University Press, 1983.

———. "The Social Context of Pauline Theology." *Interpretation* 36, no. 3 (1982): 266–77.

Meggitt, Justin J. *Paul, Poverty, and Survival*. Edinburgh: T&T Clark, 1998.

Meyer, Heinrich August Wilhelm. *Critical and Exegetical Handbook to the Epistles to the Corinthians*. Translated by D. D. Bannerman. Revised and edited by W. P. Dickson. New York, NY: Funk & Wagnalls, 1884.

Mihaila, Corin. *The Paul-Apollos Relationship and Paul's Stance towards Greco-Roman Rhetoric*. Library of New Testament Studies 402. London: T&T Clark, 2009.

Mitchell, Margaret M. "The Corinthian Correspondence and the Birth of Pauline Hermeneutics." In *Paul and the Corinthians: Studies on a Community in Conflict: Essays in Honour of Margaret Thrall*, edited by Trevor J. Burke and J. Keith Elliott, 17–54. Leiden: Brill, 2003.

———. *Paul and the Rhetoric of Reconciliation: An Exegetical Investigation of the Language and Composition of 1 Corinthians*. Louisville, KY: Westminster John Knox, 1992.

Moore, George Foot. *Judaism in the First Centuries of the Christian Era: The Age of Tannaim*. 3 vols. Peabody, MA: Hendrickson, 1997.

Muilenburg, James. "Form Criticism and Beyond." *Journal of Biblical Literature* 88, no. 1 (1969): 1–18.

Munck, Johannes. "The Church without Factions: Studies in I Corinthians 1–4." In *Christianity at Corinth: The Quest for the Pauline Church*, edited by Edward Adams and David G. Horrell, 61–70. Louisville, KY: Westminster John Knox, 2004.

———. *Paul and the Salvation of Mankind*. Richmond, VA: John Knox, 1959.

Murphy-O'Connor, Jerome. *St. Paul's Corinth: Texts and Archaeology*. Wilmington, DE: Michael Glazier, 1983.

Neyrey, Jerome H. "Social-Scientific Criticism." In *The Blackwell Companion to the New Testament*, edited by David E. Aune, 177–91. Chichester: Wiley-Blackwell, 2010.

O'Day, Gail R. "Jeremiah 9:22–23 and 1 Corinthians 1:26–31: A Study in Intertextuality." *Journal of Biblical Literature* 109, no. 2 (1990): 259–67.

Orr, William F., and James Arthur Walther. *1 Corinthians*. Anchor Bible 32. Garden City, NY: Doubleday, 1976.

Oster, Richard E., Jr. "Use, Misuse and Neglect of Archaeological Evidence in Some Modern Works in 1 Corinthians (1 Cor. 7:1–5; 8:10; 11:2–16; 12:14–26)." *Zeitschrift für die neutestamentliche Wissenschaft und die Kunde der älteren Kirche* 83, no. 1/2 (1992): 52–73.

Pearson, Birger Albert. *The Pneumatikos-Psychikos Terminology in 1 Corinthians: A Study in the Theology of the Corinthians Opponents of Paul and Its Relation to Gnosticism*. Society of Biblical Literature Dissertation Series 12. Missoula, MO: Scholars Press, 1973.

Peterson, Brian K. *Eloquence and the Proclamation of the Gospel in Corinth*. Society of Biblical Literature Dissertation Series 163. Atlanta, GA: Scholars Press, 1998.

Pickett, Raymond. *The Cross in Corinth: The Social Significance of the Death of Jesus*. Journal for the Study of the New Testament Supplement Series 143. Sheffield: Sheffield Academic, 1997.

Plummer, Robert L. "Imitation of Paul and the Church's Missionary Role in 1 Corinthians." *Journal of the Evangelical Theological Society* 44, no. 2 (2001): 219–35.

Pogoloff, Stephen M. *Logos and Sophia: The Rhetorical Situation of 1 Corinthians*. Society of Biblical Literature Dissertation Series 134. Atlanta, GA: Scholars Press, 1992.

Polhill, John B. "The Wisdom of God and Factionalism: 1 Corinthians 1–4." *Review and Expositor* 80, no. 3 (1983): 325–39.

Reed, Jeffrey T. "Using Ancient Rhetorical Categories to Interpret Paul's Letters: A Question of Genre." In *Rhetoric and the New Testament: Essays from the 1992 Heidelberg Conference*, edited by Stanley E. Porter and Thomas H. Olbricht, 292–324. Journal for the Study of the New Testament Supplement Series 90. Sheffield: Sheffield Academic Press, 1993.

Resseguie, James L. *Narrative Criticism of the New Testament: An Introduction*. Grand Rapids, MI: Baker Academic, 2005.

Saller, Richard P. *Personal Patronage under the Early Empire*. Cambridge: Cambridge University Press, 1982.

———. "Patronage and Friendship in Early Imperial Rome: Drawing the Distinction." In *Patronage in Ancient Society*, edited by Andrew Wallace-Hadrill, 49–62. London: Routledge, 1989.

Sanders, Boykin. "Imitating Paul: 1 Cor 4:16." *Harvard Theological Review* 74, no. 4 (1981): 353–64.

Sanders, G. D. R. "Urban Corinth: An Introduction." In *Urban Religion in Roman Corinth: Interdisciplinary Approaches*, edited by Daniel N. Schowalter and Steven J. Friesen, 11–24. Harvard Theological Studies 53. Cambridge, MA: Harvard University Press, 2005.

Scholer, David M., ed. *Social Distinctives of the Christians in the First Century: Pivotal Essays by E. A. Judge*. Peabody, MA: Hendrickson, 2008.

Scroggs, Robin. "Paul: ΣΟΦΟΣ and ΠΝΕΥΜΑΤΙΚΟΣ." *New Testament Studies* 14, no. 1 (1967): 33–55.

———. "The Sociological Interpretation of the New Testament: The Present State of Research." In *The Bible and Liberation: Political and Social Hermeneutics*, edited by Norman K. Gottwald, 337–56. Maryknoll, NY: Orbis Books, 1984.

Smit, Joop. "What Is Apollos? What Is Paul? In Search for the Coherence of First Corinthians 1:10–4:21." *Novum Testamentum* 44, no. 3 (2002): 231–51.

Smith, Jonathan Z. "The Social Description of Early Christianity." *Religious Studies Review* 1 (1975): 19–25.

Spawforth, Antony J. S. "Achaean Federal Court Part I." *Tyndale Bulletin* 46, no. 1 (1995): 151–68.

———. "Corinth, Argos and the Imperial Cult: Pseudo-Julian, Letters 198." *Hesperia* 63, no. 2 (1994): 211–32.

Stambaugh, John E., and David L. Balch. *The New Testament in Its Social Environment*. Philadelphia, PA: Westminster, 1986.

Ste. Croix, G. E. M., de. *The Class Struggle in the Ancient Greek World: from the Archaic Age to the Arab Conquests*. Ithaca, NY: Cornell University Press, 1981.

Steyn, G. "Reflections on τό ὄνομα τοῦ κυρίου in 1 Corinthians." In *The Corinthian Correspondence*, edited by R. Bieringer, 479–90. Leuven: Leuven University Press, 1996.

Stowers, Stanley Kent. "Social Status, Public Speaking and Private Teaching: The Circumstances of Paul's Preaching Activity." *Novum Testamentum* 26, Fasc. 1 (1984): 59–82.

Theissen, Gerd. *The Social Setting of Pauline Christianity: Essays on Corinth*. Edited and translated by John Schütz. Edinburgh: T&T Clark, 1982.

———. *Sociology of Early Palestinian Christianity*. Translated by J. Bowden. Philadelphia, PA: Fortress, 1978.

———. "The Sociological Interpretation of Religious Traditions: Its Methodological Problems as Exemplified in Early Christianity." In *The Bible and Liberation: Political and Social Hermeneutics*, edited by N. Gottwald, 38–53. Maryknoll, NY: Orbis Books, 1984.

———. *Social Reality and the Early Christians: Theology Ethics and the World of the New Testament*. Translated by Margaret Kohl. Minneapolis, MN: Fortress, 1992.

Thiselton, Anthony C. *A Commentary on First Corinthians*. New International Greek Testament Commentary. Grand Rapids, MI: Eerdmans, 2000.

Vos, Craig Steven de. *Church and Community Conflicts: The Relationship of Thessalonian, Corinthian and Philippian Churches with Their Wider Civic Communities*. Society of Biblical Literature Dissertation Series 168. Atlanta, GA: Scholars Press, 1999.

———. "Once a Slave, always a Slave? Slavery, Manumission and Relational Patterns in Paul's Letter to Philemon." *Journal for the Study of the New Testament* 23, no. 82 (2000): 89–105.

Wallace-Hadrill, Andrew. "Patronage in Roman Society: From Republic to Empire." In *Patronage in Ancient Society*, edited by Andrew Wallace-Hadrill, 63–88. London: Routledge, 1989.

Walters, James. "Civic Identity in Roman Corinth and Its Impact on Early Christians." In *Urban Religion in Roman Corinth: Interdisciplinary Approaches*, edited by Daniel N. Schowalter and Steven J. Friesen, 397–418. Harvard Theological Studies 53. Cambridge, MA: Harvard University Press, 2005.

Wanamaker, Charles. "A Rhetoric of Power: Ideology and 1 Corinthians 1–4." In *Paul and the Corinthians: Studies on a Community in Conflict: Essays in Honour of Margaret Thrall*, edited by Trevor J. Burke and J. Keith Elliott, 115–38. Leiden: Brill, 2003.

Watson, Duane Frederick. *Invention, Arrangement, and Style: Rhetorical Criticism of Jude and 2 Peter*. Society of Biblical Literature Dissertation Series 104. Atlanta, GA: Scholars Press, 1988.

———. "Three Species of Rhetoric and the Study of the Pauline Letters." In *Paul and Rhetoric*, edited by J. Paul Sampley and Peter Lampe, 25–47. New York, NY: T&T Clark, 2010.

Watson, Duane Frederick, and Allan J. Hauser. *Rhetorical Criticism of the Bible: A Comprehensive Bibliography with Notes on History and Method*. Leiden: Brill, 1994.

Welborn, Laurence L. "On the Discord in Corinth: 1 Corinthians 1–4 and Ancient Politics." *Journal of Biblical Literature* 106, no. 1 (1987): 85–111.

———. *An End to Enmity: Paul and the "Wrongdoer" of Second Corinthians*. Berlin: de Gruyter, 2011.

———. *Politics and Rhetoric in the Corinthian Epistles*. Macon, GA: Mercer University Press, 1997.

Wendland, Ernst R. "Aspects of Rhetorical Analysis Applied to New Testament Texts." In *Handbook of Early Christianity: Social Science Approaches*, edited by Anthony J. Blasi, Jeane Duhaime, and Paul-Andre Turcotte, 169–96. Walnut Creek, CA: Altamira Press, 2002.

West, Allen Brown, ed. *Corinth: Results of Excavations Conducted by The American School of Classical Studies at Athens. Vol. VIII, Part II: Latin Inscriptions: 1896–1926*. Cambridge, MA: Harvard University Press, 1931.

White, Adam G. *Where Is the Wise Man?: Graeco-Roman Education as a Background to the Divisions in 1 Corinthians 1–4*. Library of New Testament Studies 536. London: T&T Clark, 2015.

Williams, David J. *Paul's Metaphors: Their Context and Character*. Peabody, MA: Hendrickson, 1999.

Williams, H. H. Drake III. *The Wisdom of the Wise: The Presence and Function of Scripture within 1 Cor. 1:18–3:23*. Leiden: Brill, 2001.

Winter, Bruce W. "The Achaean Federal Imperial Cult Part II." *Tyndale Bulletin* 46, no. 1 (1995): 169–78.

———. *After Paul Left Corinth: The Influence of Secular Ethics and Social Change*. Grand Rapids, MI: Eerdmans, 2001.

———. *Philo and Paul Among the Sophists: Alexandrian and Corinthian Responses to a Julio-Claudian Movement*. 2d ed. Grand Rapids, MI: Eerdmans, 2002.

Witherington, Ben III. *Conflict and Community in Corinth*. Grand Rapids, MI: Eerdmans, 1995.

Woolf, Greg. "Becoming Roman, Staying Greek: Culture, Identity and the Civilizing Process in the Roman East." *Proceedings of the Cambridge Philological Society* 40 (1994): 116–43.

Wuellner, William H. "The Sociological Implications of 1 Corinthians 1:26–28 Revisited." In *Studia Evangelica*, volume 6, edited by Elizabeth A. Livingstone, 666–72. Berlin: Akademie-Verlag, 1973.

———. "Where Is Literary Criticism Taking Us?" *Catholic Biblical Quarterly* 49, no. 3 (1987): 448–63.

Langham Literature, with its publishing work, is a ministry of Langham Partnership.

Langham Partnership is a global fellowship working in pursuit of the vision God entrusted to its founder John Stott –

> *to facilitate the growth of the church in maturity and Christ-likeness through raising the standards of biblical preaching and teaching.*

Our vision is to see churches in the Majority World equipped for mission and growing to maturity in Christ through the ministry of pastors and leaders who believe, teach and live by the word of God.

Our mission is to strengthen the ministry of the word of God through:
- nurturing national movements for biblical preaching
- fostering the creation and distribution of evangelical literature
- enhancing evangelical theological education

especially in countries where churches are under-resourced.

Our ministry

Langham Preaching partners with national leaders to nurture indigenous biblical preaching movements for pastors and lay preachers all around the world. With the support of a team of trainers from many countries, a multi-level programme of seminars provides practical training, and is followed by a programme for training local facilitators. Local preachers' groups and national and regional networks ensure continuity and ongoing development, seeking to build vigorous movements committed to Bible exposition.

Langham Literature provides Majority World preachers, scholars and seminary libraries with evangelical books and electronic resources through publishing and distribution, grants and discounts. The programme also fosters the creation of indigenous evangelical books in many languages, through writer's grants, strengthening local evangelical publishing houses, and investment in major regional literature projects, such as one volume Bible commentaries like the Africa Bible Commentary and the South Asia Bible Commentary.

Langham Scholars provides financial support for evangelical doctoral students from the Majority World so that, when they return home, they may train pastors and other Christian leaders with sound, biblical and theological teaching. This programme equips those who equip others. Langham Scholars also works in partnership with Majority World seminaries in strengthening evangelical theological education. A growing number of Langham Scholars study in high quality doctoral programmes in the Majority World itself. As well as teaching the next generation of pastors, graduated Langham Scholars exercise significant influence through their writing and leadership.

To learn more about Langham Partnership and the work we do visit langham.org

www.ingramcontent.com/pod-product-compliance
Lightning Source LLC
Chambersburg PA
CBHW071742150426
43191CB00010B/1666